When You Lie About Your Age,
the Terrorists Win

VILLARD / NEW YORK

When You Lie About Your Age, the Terrorists Win

Reflections on Looking in the Mirror

CAROL LEIFER

Published in the United States by Villard Books, an imprint of The
Random House Publishing Group, a division of Random House, Inc.,
New York.

VILLARD and "V" CIRCLED Design are registered trademarks of
Random House, Inc.

Library of Congress Cataloging-in-Publication Data

Leifer, Carol.
When you lie about your age, the terrorists win / Carol Leifer.
p. cm.
ISBN 978-0-345-50296-4
1. Leifer, Carol.   2. Comedians—United States—Biography.
3. Television comedy writers—United States—Biography.   I. Title.

PN2287.L337A 2009
792.702'8092—dc22   2008056024
[B]

Printed in the United States of America on acid-free paper

www.villard.com

4 6 8 9 7 5 3

Book design by Susan Turner

For Lori and Bruno

Cheer up. Life isn't everything.

—MIKE NICHOLS

Contents

When You Lie About Your Age,
the Terrorists Win

But This One's
Eating My Popcorn

My father was a really funny guy. He lived a good long life. And he was the reason I wanted to be funny and become a comedian and a comedy writer, so to say that he's somewhat of a mythic figure in my life would be an understatement. Every year, I sent my father the same thing, his favorite gift for his birthday. A box of Godiva chocolate-covered nuts. Big emphasis on the nuts. Because, as he was not shy of saying as he unwrapped the cellophane to grab the first piece, "Creams? They're a waste of time."

But this year is the first year I have no place to send anything. See, that's the thing that truly sucks about death—no forwarding address. So on this birthday, which would have been his eighty-seventh, in lieu of a gold box of chocolates, hopefully this story will come in a close second.

I have very clear, distinct memories of looking up to my father holding court and telling jokes when I was a little girl. And for the record? I see now that as a child a lot of "looking up to your parents" has to do with height. So my father would tell jokes mostly at family gatherings or with people around the neighborhood, and I was fascinated by the power of him telling these stories. Now, don't forget that when you're a kid, stories are major. A big chunk of your life revolves around them. Granted, they're mostly about princesses and fairy godmothers, moonbeams and farm animals, but that's pretty much your iPod at that age. And here was this guy, my relative yet, telling very short stories to people who were standing up—not in bed in their pajamas. Revolutionary! Then at the end of this very short story, he would say this one line, a little more forcefully and pointedly than the rest of the story, and everybody would roar. But that one line was usually when he lost me.

What I came to find out was that these were the punch lines to "dirty" jokes being told. And I learned to distinguish them from clean jokes, because as he approached the punch line—the mystery line to me—the circle around him became that much tighter and smaller.

Here's a joke I remember my father telling a lot. "A guy goes to the ticket window of a movie theater with a chicken on his shoulder and asks for two tickets. The ticket lady asks who's going in with him, and the guys says, 'My pet chicken here.' 'Well, I'm sorry,' the woman tells him, 'but we don't allow animals in the movie theater.' So the guy goes around the corner and stuffs the chicken down his pants. He goes back to the window, buys his ticket, and goes into the theater. But once the movie begins, the chicken starts to get hot, so the guy unzips his pants so the chicken can stick his head out and get a little air. The woman sitting next to the guy in the movies sees this and is appalled. She nudges her friend and whispers, 'This guy next to me just unzipped his pants!' The friend whispers back, 'Ah, don't worry about it. You've seen one, you've seen them all.' And the woman says, 'I know. But this one's eating my popcorn!'"

Now, as a little girl, the bulk of this joke made sense. "Chicken"—sure, I was made to eat that quite a bit. "Chicken as a pet"—never seen it, but I'd buy it; I'd just bought "a cow jumping over the moon" the previous night. "Movies"—fun, mostly when they were cartoons. "Popcorn"—love it, but to get those two tightwads I lived with to spring for any outside of the house, good luck. But then that damn punch line! What gives? My older brother alluded to it being a penis joke, but all I heard mentioned was a chicken and a zipper. Forget "Why did the chicken cross the road?" How did the chicken become a schmeckle?! So there was always this mystery to comedy when I was a kid that made it so appealing to me.

But besides jokes, my father was just naturally funny. He had his version of the world and he always felt things should be done in a certain way. Kind of like the *Farmer's Almanac,* but the Jewish edition. Like when we would go to Fortunoff, a popular home store on Long Island, he would park the car really far away in the lot. "You see, this way, nobody dings your car and I get a good walk in." Or his philosophy on weight gain: "When my pants start to feel a little snug, I cut out the cake at night."

I remember once when I was trying to get my parents to come out to L.A. to visit me, I offered to buy them plane tickets. My father was adamant, "No, no!" "Dad, look, if you come out, I'll buy you a first-class ticket." My incredulous father said, "Carol. *First class?* We're not drinkers!"

Or when AIDS was first happening in the early eighties and I was at my folks' house watching a news piece on it, and my father said, "I don't understand how it gets into the bloodstream." And I said—quite uncomfortably, I might add—"Dad. From anal sex." And my father goes, "Anal sex? Carol, they don't go in there! They simply rest it gently in between the buttocks." His conception of gay sex was basically a hot dog in a bun.

My father also had an offbeat, quirky way of phrasing things. Like when it was really cold outside, he would say, "It refuses to get warmer." Not "It won't get warmer." It "refuses." Or if he wanted all the info for an event, he would say, "Give me the particulars." "Particulars." Or when he said his favorite phrase to just about anything disappointing that happened in our lives, "I maintain that everything happens for the best." "I maintain." It's just so much better than "I say" or "I believe."

My father also had a great facility with the "callback" joke. When my marriage many years ago was falling apart, my mother was in complete denial about it. I would call my folks for our weekly Sunday chat, and my mother would invariably interject into the conversation, "And how are the

Shydners?" which would make my father lose it. "Anne, they're splitting up! Stop asking about the Shydners!" So for many years after that, whenever someone made any kind of inane comment, my father would always say, "Yeah, and how are the Shydners?"

My shrink says it's important not to deify someone when they die, but he's a killjoy who has to open his big fat trap about everything. But lest I get too sentimental, my father could also, at times, be a really insensitive know-it-all. I once played the Westbury Music Fair opening for Jay Leno, and it was quite a big deal. This was my "hometown" theater, and I can't tell you how thrilling it is playing the place where, growing up, I'd seen the Carpenters, Gladys Knight and the Pips, and six different versions of the Beach Boys, among others. My father came along to the gig with me, and it was really cool. They had a sign backstage welcoming us and generally made a big fuss over him. I went on and had a great set, and I was ecstatic.

Now, at the time, I was doing this joke about how I had been married for four years, and how the gift for that anniversary is wood. The joke being "Honey, I know you had your eye on that antique necklace, but, heck, you're so special, I got you twenty yards of one-by-eight." So when my father saw me after I came offstage, the first thing he said to me was, "Carol, lumber is sold in feet, not in yards." Not "Congratulations." Not "You killed!" It was one of those things where he just couldn't help himself, unfortunately. (Little footnote to this story—the next day, our local newspaper, *Newsday*, did a review of the show and favorably reviewed Jay and panned me. My father read the review and said, as any good Jew would, "The reviewer is clearly anti-Semitic!")

My father was an optometrist for sixty years, and he enjoyed his professional life. He never lived his dream of becoming a comedian or a comedy writer. But he was really happy for me that I did, and I never felt one pang of resentment or jealousy from him (the lumber joke notwithstanding). The first time I did the Letterman show, he said he "cried like a baby" when he saw my name listed in the TV section of *The New York Times*. But whenever I feel bad that my father never got to make it professionally, I think about what everyone says to me when they find out that he died. They always say, "He was so funny." And I think if my father could know that being funny is the first thing people say about him, that would be enough and make him really happy. I know it makes me happy.

Obviously, at this age, I've lost people in my life. But with a parent, it's just different. I was very attached to my father and had this naïve little-girl notion that he'd always be around. So I'm finding acceptance of my father's death is, ironically, the hardest thing to accept.

See, I'm one of those people who don't take no for an answer well. A big kicker and screamer from way back. You want your money back for something? You want some kind of compensation for some bad treatment somewhere? I'm your girl! But that's what stinks about this whole death experience. There's no manager to ask for. Well, I guess that technically would be God, but come on, he's got more important stuff on his "to do" list than coming down to customer service for this.

I do wonder whether I'll get to see my father again. I'm sure most people wonder about this when someone they really love dies. But my father was very matter-of-fact about death. I know he believed that when you go, you go. Heaven was for gentiles. But if he's wrong, then I think he'll be sorry that he didn't make a plan with me. 'Cause a plan would have been right up his alley. "Carol. When you get here, there's got to be an information booth of some type. So meet me to the left of it. Not right in front of it. That's where everybody will go. Left. No, facing-the-booth left! And when I see you and kiss that punim of yours, I'll give you the rest of the particulars."

40 Things I Know at 50
(Because 50 Is the New 40)

1. The people who frequent nude beaches are never the people you want to see naked.
2. Making love to a woman is like buying real estate— "Location, location, location!"
3. Never buy expensive thong underwear. One trip through the dryer and it's a frilly bookmark.
4. Never put your baby's length on a birth announcement. It's a baby, not a marlin.
5. If you see a woman with a big belly, never ask if she's pregnant or when she's due. Trust me.
6. If you have a garage sale at your house, don't be afraid to put anything and everything out. (I once sold half a bottle of Listerine.)

7. Never eat pistachio nuts after getting a French manicure.

8. When someone says, "To make a long story short," they're already too late.

9. When a waiter asks you to taste the wine and you're clueless, sip it and then say, "Yeah, that should get me hammered."

10. Badly cut bangs do always grow back.

11. A great birthday gift for a woman you don't like who's about to turn forty? Magnifying mirror.

12. Best job for a woman? Judge. She gets to wear a big black weight-hiding muumuu all day.

13. Worst job for a woman? Naval recruit. How anyone would have the courage to wear white pants all year is beyond me.

14. When someone starts a sentence with "No offense . . . ," you can bet they are about to say something incredibly offensive. (Same goes for "Nothing personal . . ." and "Can I give you some constructive criticism?")

15. Tequila should always be sold with an instant camera attached to it so the next day you have some idea of what happened.

16. Five-minute drum solos are always four and a half minutes too long.

17. The phrase "good toupee" is an oxymoron.

18. I believe that we can take the word "morbidly" out of the phrase "morbidly obese." It seems mean and gratuitous, like calling someone stroke-inducingly plain.

19. Worst question to ask an elderly person? "How are you feeling?" You'll be there for days. (Second worst question? "I'm sorry, could you repeat that?")
20. Someone named Adolph has a hard time dating.
21. When a salesperson in a clothing store tells you that you look great in something, always remember that they work on commission.
22. The sunny side of the street is the one with the threat of skin cancer on it.
23. Never wear high heels to an event if you're going to be outside on a lawn.
24. If your thighs make noise while wearing corduroy pants, you need to lose some weight.
25. If you can tie a cherry stem with your tongue, you are really good at sex.
26. A witch's tit is not colder than anyone else's tit.
27. When your husband suggests experimenting sexually with multiple "inputs," politely remind him that you are a woman and not a surge protector.
28. Never refer to a woman as "ma'am," even if she's ninety years old. No one likes it.
29. You may not rationalize eating an entire pint of ice cream by claiming it was for the calcium.
30. Never eat at a restaurant that charges for bread.
31. No one looks good eating a burrito. Not even a porn actress.
32. A fly in an airplane is very lost.
33. Men recuperate from the death of a spouse much sooner than women do.

34. When you offer someone a mint, they will invariably ask, "Why, do I need one?"

35. Never buy Sweet'N Low, Equal, or Splenda at the supermarket. That's what restaurants are for.

36. If you plan on having your lover's name tattooed on your arm, always leave room before it for a possible "I Hate" down the road.

37. Why do men have nipples? What's the point? They're like plastic fruit.

38. Professional bodybuilders look like walking challahs.

39. Never complain about your age to someone older than you.

40. Director Norman Jewison is ironically not Jewish.

Shea Stadium and Its Effect on the Aging Process

It starts around the age of forty-five—when the only time people say you're young anymore is if you drop dead. Getting older is hard—there's no way around it. Your life starts being written in pen where it was once in pencil.

I thought briefly about lying about my age. Please, it's almost a prerequisite for women at this point. And it would have been a very easy plan to implement, as well. Friends tell me that I don't look my age, thanks to good genes and insane slatherings with sunblock. But then recently it came up again, and I realized why the lying was a no-go: Shea Stadium. Yes, blame the grande dame of Flushing for the blazing light that is the truth of my age. See, my greatest memory to date happened at Shea Stadium—and no, it wasn't when

I was briefly on the roster in 1986 and stole home off of Roger Clemens in the World Series.

It was in the summer of 1966, at Shea Stadium, where I saw the Beatles. I was ten years old and went with my older brother, Marv, who was twenty-one and home from college—and who felt like going *on the same day.* Pretty wild, huh? Nothing has been as exciting to me ever. Yeah, I know, I could be all gooey and say the most exciting day was the one I met the love of my life, or the first time I laid eyes on our son, but I'd just be fibbing, even though those two days were really quite perfect. No, it's the Fab Four. We drove there in my brother's white 1964 Sunbeam convertible with the top down. We got great seats. I sang along to every song, being a rabid Beatles fan at the time because of my older sister and brother. I screamed my lungs out. I got to stay up late. But mostly, I was part of it. I was in it. I experienced the greatest rock band of the twentieth century, live—at an incredibly pure and impressionable age. *Now* tell me about the time you shook hands with Batman at the car show!

So not surprisingly, this memory blows people away. But lately I've noticed, pretty soon after the blowing away is over and long gone to bed, a number of people then remark, "The Beatles. . . . Jesus Christ! How old *are* you?" See, you can't tell this story without revealing your age. In fact, it's to my *advantage* to tell people my age 'cause I went as such a young kid. So it got me thinking—if I can't share the greatest memory of my life to date, then what *do* I share? Because I see now that when you deny your age, you deny yourself. And when you lie about your age, you become your inauthentic twin. But most important, when you lie about your age, they win. (And of course by "they," I mean the terrorists.)

I remember crying when I turned thirty-four. For no other reason than thirty-four seemed "old." That seems pretty dumb seventeen years later. And that's exactly the problem I feel with aging. We're getting older every moment. I'm older now than when I first brought up those damn Mop Tops. So why latch on to a problem that only gets worse with every passing second?

And if you're a woman like me—like the vast majority of women—who has never made her living off her looks, revel in the odometer! I think of all those glamour pusses along the way who are seriously having a hard time now. They weren't very nice to us regular-looking folk, now, were they? With their derisive sneers in group dressing rooms, their noses in the air as they glided into nightclubs while we shivered outside. I eat it up like the hot fudge sundae they still haven't had. Life isn't very fun now, is it, pretty girl? When you don't turn heads anymore and yours still just bobbles? Kinda sucks, when you made sure to hit all those beauty appointments, but never once stopped at a library. Geez, having a conversation is *hard*!

If I've learned one thing about getting older, it's this: Don't fight it. "Anti-aging"? State-driven propaganda. The only thing that is truly anti-aging is death.

So here's my aging advice, for what it's worth, and I think it works wonders. It's not the latest cream or the name of a doctor who did some work on some celebrity who doesn't look like she's had anything done. No, it's two things that I feel can make this a whole lot easier for you, so listen carefully. Number one: No one gives a crap how old you are except for you. Didn't think so, did ya? But it's true. You are your own greatest accountant (especially if you're Jewish).

And number two is merely a couple of sentences, Grasshopper, that if you accept—*truly* accept—will make the rest of your life a whole lot better. And here it goes: This ends. We end. I can hear you out there saying, "But I already know that, smart-ass lady writer!" But do you? Then why are you getting an eye job when eyes are supposed to crinkle up on the sides when you laugh? Why are you cutting and pasting when the tread on a tire is supposed to show some wear? If you're fifty-three, your face ain't supposed to look sixteen.

Again, this ends. We end. And I know your religious beliefs may tell you otherwise. I know mine do. But for now, this is all we know. So you can go on fighting it, and crying over it, but really, what's the use? Accept and deal. And it's easier to grasp than you think. We accept "the end" with so many other aspects of our lives—work deadlines, "must remit by" bills, "the end" as the last credit on a movie. But for some reason we still think somewhere that we're supposed to be here forever. Believe me, I once thought so, too. But losing a parent changes that. I guess it's the old food chain thing—when a link is missing and you're the next one up, that's some pretty powerful stuff.

So give this a whirl. You know when you book that vacation you've always dreamed about? For me, it was Maui. And you plan every waking second to make full use of being in this wonderland that only existed up till now in your head? It's a Sunday to Sunday trip. And there's no getting around it—your return flight is booked, with severe penalties for changing it. And even if you wanted to stay longer, they're sold out at the hotel, so that's not even possible. You don't fight it, you just enjoy and accept it. And life to me is that week in Maui. You just soak up the number of days you have and wring every last drop out of 'em. Yes, aging sucks. But so does day number seven of seven days in Maui.

If I haven't changed your mind yet, here's another thing that will sober you right up and stop you from obsessing about getting older—friends who are no longer here. By this age, you've lost a few. For me, it's been two female comedy buddies who I worked with closely. It didn't happen suddenly; they had to sit with it for a while. And I was privy to their personal horror at knowing they were leaving here at forty and forty-four. What they would give to be back here. Wrinkled, gray, with a huge ass, sporting a goiter, whatever. *What they would give to be back.* And when I find I'm feeling sorry for myself because my triceps are a little jiggly or my abs are nowhere to be found, it all seems incredibly trite and embarrassing in light of their absence. Shame on me.

Be who you are—memories and all. Enjoy your life. It ends. We end. Getting older is supposed to happen. Okay, so my rack isn't as high as it used to be. But guess what? They're mine and they didn't come from a box and there's no chance the FDA might recall them. I'm here, and if my calculations are correct, it's around day five for me in Maui. The sun is shining, the breeze is blowing—I'm drinking a mai tai and listening to "Day Tripper," remembering when I saw the lads from Liverpool *play that song*. And the best part is—I've still got two days left! So what else will I do here in my paradise?

Surprise!

"If I don't sleep with a woman soon, I think I'll kill myself."

That's what I remember saying to my buddy Ed on the golf course right before this all happened. (And yes, I'm well aware of the irony that this plea was uttered on a golf course.)

I was eager. I was pumped. "I'm ready for my lesbian fling, Mr. DeMille!" Turning forty does that to you. You feel like Father Time has gotten a second wind and is catching up. Suddenly everything you wanted to try or experiment with has to be done in this short period called "midlife"— before you reach that next stage in life, the one where you don't care if you go to the supermarket in your pajamas.

"I want to learn how to operate a potter's wheel!"

"I want to enroll in salsa boot camp!"

"Me? I just wanna get it on with a lady!"

Forget that I'd already been married and had only dated men my entire life. It didn't matter, because when you feel that sapphic siren call, there is no backing down. And before I knew it, as if in a dream, this vision appeared right before my very eyes. It was a Saturday night and I was at a Project Angel Food charity dinner with some gay male friends. There she sat, right across from my two-hundred-dollar plate.

Her name was Lori. Blond, gorgeous, obviously sophisticated—what the young people at the time were calling a "lipstick lesbian." There was only one small catch—she was with a date. And you couldn't help but notice that they were quite frisky with each other, starting with the appetizers.

Amid their flirting, I made a stab at some tiny small talk about—you guessed it—golf. And she was polite, friendly, and couldn't have been less interested in me. But I was on my midlife mission. I called our mutual friend the following Monday.

"David, I met that gal at our table Saturday night, and I think I have a crush on her."

"Yeah, but she's dating that woman."

"I know. But I need my lesbian fling!"

"Well, I hate to break this to ya, sweetheart," he said, "but much like in the straight world, when someone is already in a relationship, it's better to pursue someone else who isn't."

"I don't care. I'm so attracted to her. Can you call her up and suggest that we maybe play some golf together?"

And without a moment's hesitation, he got on the phone immediately. Why? Because this stuff is like crack to a gay man.

We met a week later at the Par 3 in Studio City (which sounds like a lesbian bar, doesn't it?) and she was even prettier in her casual hitting-the-links wear.

"I'm so glad David made this happen," she said. "I don't have a lot of friends right now who play golf."

Well, this one does, baby girl, I thought.

"You look like you work out," Lori said. "Do you? You've got such a nice tight waist."

Ooooh, is someone flirting with Mommy and we haven't even teed off yet? I got to the meat of the matter. "So how's your girlfriend? The one I saw a couple weeks back at the Angel Food dinner?"

"Oh, we broke up."

Yes. "Oh, that's sad," I lied. "I'm so very sorry."

"Oh, don't be. Wasn't meant to be. So what's your story, Carol? Why aren't you in a relationship?"

"I don't know. I'm going through some stuff right now."

"Oh, really? Well, we can turn that around in no time flat."

Gulp! Maybe my lesbionic vibe was more transparent than I'd thought! "H-how's that?" I stuttered.

"Well, there are a million guys at my office I could set you up with, no problem!"

And suddenly, someone on my same-sex train pulled the emergency stop. We played the round, and I spent the better part of it cursing (and alternately blessing) my straight-girl demeanor.

So I proceeded to code blue. I called David. "Buddy, before my midlife crisis becomes my mid-to-later-life crisis, let's go for broke. Just tell her I have a crush on her and see what happens."

And like any good crack addict, he did. But I was not happy with his report back: "Lori told me she wasn't going to be some science experiment for a straight girl."

Not even for extra credit? I thought.

But there was no denying it. I was busted.

Well, I'd tried. And salsa boot camp did sound pretty fun. So my dream of a lesbian dalliance went out in a puff of smoke. Oh, well, I could still rent the movie *Bound* another thousand times!

That's how it was, until a few weeks later when she called and left a message on my machine: "Hi. It's Lori. It's Sunday and I feel like hitting some golf balls at the driving range. If you're up for it, gimme a call."

And I immediately . . . didn't call back. Straight or gay, I'd read that book *The Rules* (or at least seen the authors talk about it on TV). She already knew I was an easy catch. Why help her reel me in? Then, a few days later, I got another call from her at my office.

"How spontaneous are you?" she asked.

Bingo!

"I have an empty seat at my company's table tonight for the Beverly Hills policeman's ball over at the Beverly Hilton. Feel like coming along?"

"Sure. As long as they don't arrest us for what's gonna happen to you afterward." (I didn't actually say that last part, but I sure thought it.)

So off we went to help raise money for the men in blue of Beverly Hills, so they could all upgrade their bulletproof vests to Gucci ones. The drinking started early. (Doesn't it always?) Then the drinking moved over to Trader Vic's and it all came tumbling out.

"So come on, Lady Lesbian. What's up with you?"

"Look," she said, "getting involved with a straight girl is dangerous."

And then I pulled out my patented line that I have used easily for a good twenty years. (And folks, feel free to use it, please.) On men, women, whoever—doesn't matter—it's truly fail-safe. Here's the line:

"Well, what would it hurt if we just made out?"

I'm telling you, no one ever passes up this line. Because if you start making out and it sucks, it will stop right there—no harm, no foul. But if it's fantastic, which in this case it was, suit up, because someone's gonna be rounding some bases.

But surprisingly, that's not where it ended that night. I'd always rushed to sleep with guys before this, but for my lesbian fling it just felt right to take it slow.

She promised to call me the next morning, and lo and behold, she did. Hmm, these chicks are trustworthy! She said she was going to the Beverly Center mall the next day. I said I had a pair of sneakers to return there, and she offered to do it for me. My heart melted. (Strange, though, how if she had been a guy and had offered to return my sneakers, I think it would've been sort of weird and creepy.)

She was going away in a couple of weeks for the Christmas holidays to Hawaii and asked me to come along. Did I even have to think about it? If you're gonna consummate your relationship, what better place than where the breezes are tropical?

Upon arriving at the front desk of our hotel, we were confronted with the ultimate dyke detector question: "Ladies, two queens or one king bed?"

"One king, please," I said. "And we will be wanting to make some tee times as well." (Golf is never that far away.)

And as we entered the room, myself all giddy with homoerotic anticipation, the bellman suddenly decided to get oddly chatty.

"Would you like this garment bag hung in the closet or down here on the luggage rack?"

Whatever, dude, I thought. *Roll it up into a little ball and toss it at this point. I don't care.*

But he pressed on, clueless. Noticing Lori's big giant scuba diving bag, and without one iota of irony, he then said, "You girls planning on doing any diving while you're down here?"

You have no idea, buddy. You have no idea.

And so, my lesbian fling finally took flight. And sex with a woman? Turns out, it was a no-brainer . . . because I am one. (Very familiar with the equipment already.) It was like having the answers before taking a test. Like walking around in the house you grew up in. You can turn all the lights off, I'll still know where everything is.

But then something else began to happen—something I hadn't quite planned on. It started to get serious. And the next thing you know:

Surprise! You're gay!

Wait a second, this wasn't supposed to get out of control.

Too late. It did. You're gay!

It's just that, this feels so easy, so right.

Yes. Because you're a homo!

Seems like my fling had become a bona fide thing. And then the not-so-fun part was ushered in . . . coming to terms with it.

I went to gay bookstores for help. "Yes, do you have a book called *What the Fuck Just Happened to Me?!?*" I didn't understand. I'd always liked boys since I was little. My first crush was on Davy Jones of the Monkees. But then, there had been that Herb Alpert album cover of a naked woman smothered in whipped cream that I stared at much too long. And I was a bit obsessed with Patty Duke from *The Patty Duke Show*, too. Had that been a crush as well? Who knows? All I knew was I'd even had a one-night experience back in the day with my then boyfriend and another female, and it had been pleasant but certainly not something I had had any interest in doing again. In fact, I had had a lot of really good kick-ass sex with men over the years.

Doesn't matter now—you're gay!

Telling my parents . . . I knew that was going to be the big test. So I scheduled a trip to go back to New York. And my older Jewish parents from Long Island took it like champs. *I* was the one who was the basket case, all upset and crying.

"Why are you crying?" my father asked.

"Well," I sobbed, "I thought you'd be . . . disappointed."

"Disappointed?" my father said. "I'll tell you when I was disappointed. When you married that shagitz!" (For you non-Jews, a shagitz is the male version of your species.)

So here I am, twelve years later, telling you this story. This relationship has been the longest and best relationship of my life. I was afraid to talk about it for a good long while because I kept thinking it might end. And you don't want to pull an Anne Heche, sheepishly heading back to the car dealership—"Sorry. Turns out I *do* prefer a stick after all. . . ."

Granted, it's been something of an adjustment. Two menstrual cycles in one relationship? That's a keg of dynamite waiting to explode. But to me, easily, the toughest thing about being in a relationship with a woman? Getting a word in edgewise. Do you have any idea what it's like when *two people* want to talk about their day?

Love happens. Gay happens. But in the end, love always trumps the gay part. No, I didn't plan on this move to the Island of Lesbos, but I do admit that the van got there way before I did. The nice thing is, you can have anything surprising happen in your life, as long as you've got supportive friends and family. And I do. In spades.

Surprisingly, this story never seems to get old, especially to my straight male friends. I have to say that they were there for me right from the beginning—"Carol, I want to hear everything. Slowly and in great detail, please."

Sticking with Gravity

MISSION STATEMENT TO MY FACE

"To wake up every morning and have you be a gentle reminder of myself. For you to never scare or confuse me. To
look in the mirror and always be able to say, 'Hey! I know
you!'"

Bette Davis put it best—"Growing old ain't for sissies."
You said it, sister! So I want to get some things down on
paper about plastic surgery and how I feel about it. Because
the good news is, I don't need it quite yet. But the not-so-
good news is, one day I will. And, damn, do I want to make
that an informed decision! So what better time to do it than
when I'm clear, strong, and relatively supple? And when the
question comes up, I'll have some sanity written down in

black and white. A hard copy for the angel on my shoulder to shake in the face of the devil sitting on the other one. So here are the five reasons why I'm currently anti-scalpel.

1. PEOPLE DON'T COME OUT SO GOOD

I live in Los Angeles, the plastic surgery capital of the world, so I've seen a sizable chunk of the old nip and tuck. And I have to say, on a daily basis I pass way more of "What the hell did that person do to themselves?!?" than "Huh, that seemed like a good idea!"

First off, it feels like the phrase "less is more" should be the mantra chanted in a plastic surgeon's office. But, oh, quite the contrary. The norm is dialing features up to eleven that just needed maybe one more notch or two. For example, brow lifts are very popular with gals my age. And I'm no stranger to taking my two fingers and simulating that effect in the mirror, and it looks so very nice! But for those who've gone the surgery route, the execution never seems to match up to the plans. All I see are brows that took too big a trip. No longer the protective big brothers of the eyes, they're now the juvenile delinquents living fast and dangerous with the in crowd on the forehead.

And the same goes for those injections to the lips to make them fuller, poutier. Inevitably someone goes on a collagen bender. Last I checked, your lips are not meant to be the flotation devices for your face in case it capsizes.

So in a nutshell, I'm deathly afraid of winding up a plus size when all I went in for was a demure little size two.

2. THE SURGEON IS A STRANGER AND WILL ALWAYS BE

"Why is this a problem? Most of my doctors *are* strangers," you're probably saying. (Unless you're Jewish. In which case, many of your doctors are like family and attend your break-fast after Yom Kippur.)

Yes, your well-researched MD might have his degree from X Esteemed University and be on the board of Plastic Whatever, but he doesn't know you from Adam (or Eve). And this fact should be taken into consideration when it comes to slicing and dicing the only face you've got. An hour in consultation does not even begin to give him the panoply of expressions that are you. How your lip turns down slightly on the right side when you know in your gut that someone is lying. Or how your left cheek plumps out like a ripe cherry when you receive an unexpected compliment.

Personally, I've been told that when I'm asked to do something that I clearly don't want to, my face blurts out "no" way before my mouth does.

It's quite the instrument, this face of ours. And it's one Stradivarius in need of a fine fiddle player. So when that surgeon wields *his* instrument, I think it's reasonable to ask, "Does he know what makes me *me*?" (Hell, you don't even know what makes you you—because you're on the inside!) So it's really those audience members of our faces who have the most to lose from our cosmetic procedures.

This surgeon might be taking away, without your knowledge, your greatest hits. Why deprive your friends and family of the facial jukebox that is you?

3. LOOKING OLDER ALWAYS TRUMPS LOOKING DIFFERENT

I'm sure, like me, this instant you can think of any number of celebrities who went the way of the scalpel and got it really, really wrong. The ones who, when you see them on TV or in a film, you don't even recognize anymore because the work is so bad. Like they went out and made themselves their "wax museum" version a little too early.

I'm always left thinking, *Why didn't they just leave themselves alone?* And it makes me really sad because celebrities are kind of ours. And I think that they have a responsibility to stay somewhat recognizable. Like, "How can I go see your movies if I don't know what you look like anymore?" And it's precisely at times like this when what I've always suspected is absolutely confirmed—better to be yourself and aged than look like somebody else, any day.

4. MY FACE IS MY OLD PAL

At my age, I can say with some confidence that I've been around awhile. And my face has been there for all of it. I'm really used to her—flaws and all, we're buds, we're pals. Plus, the older I get, our relationship gets that much more deep. We've gone through so much together.

Sure, everyone has some feature, regardless of age, that they'd like to change about their face. If I asked you right now what that feature is for you, I bet you would have an immediate answer.

For me, it's my chin. It's a bit on the pronounced side.

For example, I know if I happen to stroll by a caricaturist on the boardwalk of some summer resort, guaranteed he will do a drawing of me that's 100 percent chin. And whatever hobby I tell him I'm into, he will draw my chin doing it. My chin riding a bike, my chin Rollerblading. (He'll also draw me off balance in whatever activity because of the ginormous boobs he's sure to give me, too. But I'm not complaining about those right now. Or ever, really.)

And it doesn't bug me that he draws me this way, because lo these many years, I've developed a bit of a soft spot for my chin. And if I ever did anything at this point to change it, it would be like losing my goofy but lovable vaudeville partner. The one who knows what bit we're launching into next just by the glint of an eye.

Besides, there's some history here as well. I come from a long line of pronounced chins. My mother has one, and apparently my great-grandma Sarah had one, and her mother, too. So who am I to mess with a dynasty? Besides, I couldn't bear to hear that gossip-fest among the clouds. Tsk-tsking and shaking their heads in the afterworld—"So Miss Big Shot doesn't like our hand-me-down?"

5. TAKING CARE OF YOURSELF DESERVES SOME PROPS

I put a lot of effort into how I look—inside and out. From the day I turned thirty, I don't think I've ever left my house without a good coat of sunblock. Eight glasses of water a day? For amateurs, sweetheart. Minimum of ten for yours truly. I don't smoke and I try to eat well, because I know it reflects in your skin and appearance. Look, I'm no saint, and I'm well aware that a heaping bowl of french fries with three vodka-tinis is never going to do my waist or my complexion any favors. But that's the exception. I try a lot, and I think it's working. You are the architect of this aging plan. You're the boss, and there is so much you can do without bringing in outside vendors.

So for my next birthday, and I hope for many more, I believe I'll still stick with gravity. "As is" is just as fine a credo for the face as it is for the discount bin. And when I get a wrinkle here or there? No biggie. At least I know I made it. There's some pride of ownership to this factory. And that laugh line? Well, take a good guess how I got it.

Dr. Me may not be licensed to practice, but damn, she's good. And I'd love to give you her number, but she likes to keep her practice small.

Extreme Makeover:
The Chanukah Edition

Being a person of the Jewish persuasion ("persuasion"? I don't recall anyone ever *cajoling* me into my faith), I celebrate Chanukah. Poor little Chanukah. The perennial also-ran of the holiday season. Want proof? Just go to any greeting card aisle in a drugstore in December. Rows and rows of Christmas cards, with maybe one and a half vertical aisles, if you're lucky, for Chanukah. And it's like a Polish ghetto! A card here, but no envelope. Three blue envelopes, but no card. Face it, the only winter holiday Chanukah's got bragging rights over is funky little Kwanzaa.

Okay, so maybe it's been thousands of years, but isn't it time to take a fresh look at our little eight-day Festival of Lights? Size it up? Throw some well-meaning constructive criticism its way? There's nothing us gals appreciate more than a good old-fashioned makeover, so why not for a holiday? Better late than never, nu?

Well, right off the bat, Chanukah is spelled a number of ways. There's the version with the *ch,* Chanukah. There's the one with no *c,* Hanukah. Some spellings have two *n*'s— the list goes on and on. Birthday of Christ? One spelling. So let's take a lesson from the king daddy of them all and agree on one universal spelling. Jews especially will love this, as we always like to know (and subsequently fight over) the absolute "correct" answer.

Right on the heels of the spelling question, even more confusion arises with Chanukah's date, as it's never on the same night every year. Whereas, Christmas? December twenty-fifth, rain or shine, folks! Chanukah—some years you barely have the drumstick out of your mouth from Thanksgiving when someone shouts "Hey, Happy Chanukah!" Then, other years, you're in Puerto Rico over Christmas week when Armando, poolside, spritzes you with Evian, hands you a piña colada, and says, "Chappy Chaaaanukah." Uniform date—I vote for that.

And what I'd like to know is, who determines the Jewish calendar anyway? Who makes *that* call every year? I bet it's just a bunch of yentas who gather once a year at the Carnegie Deli in New York City. "Well, I would like Chanukah to be around Thanksgiving this year, because my Mindy is coming in from Brandeis. And I don't know if I've mentioned it or not, but she's gotten a 4.0 so far this year!" "Well, I don't know about that date, Miriam, because my

Mel is having a procedure around then, so I would prefer Chanukah to be around the tenth of December, when he is scheduled to be released from Lenox Hill Hospital."

Now let's take a look at the symbols of Chanukah—another problematic area, I would offer. We have the menorah, our Jewish candelabra. My preference in menorahs harkens back to my childhood—the white plastic number with the screw-in orange lightbulbs. All the significance with none of the fire hazard. The second symbol of Chanukah would of course be the dreidel, which is, needless to say, tons of fun. Let me tell you, PlayStation 3's got nothing over that delightful little spinning top! And the third symbol of Chanukah—well, this one's really got me steamed—Chanukah gelt. Little chocolate coins, little chocolate money. Good idea! Let's take the worst stereotype possible about Jews and make a chocolate version of it. "Oh, look, honey. Chocolate money! The thing that Jews love!" Come on, if you want chocolo-size something, let's flaunt our assets. Make a little chocolate Barbra Streisand or Neil Diamond, perhaps?

But don't get me wrong. Even though I'm having a little fun, taking the mickey out of Chanukah, I would still never be like those turncoat Jews who celebrate Christmas. Uh-uh. No way. With their "Chanukah bushes" sitting in their living rooms? Please. Give it up. It's a Christmas tree, and you know it. Those people are in serious denial—Christmas is a party we're just not invited to. So you can quit hanging around the velvet rope, your name ain't on the list.

Gentiles don't run out to celebrate our holidays, so why

should we celebrate theirs? I mean, how many non-Jews do you know who are just clamoring to celebrate Shavuous? I'm very touchy about this subject. The worst offenders, I feel, are Jews for Jesus. Mostly because, to me, it's an oxymoron. Jews for Jesus. That's like vegans for Burger King. Lesbians for trouser meat. You get the picture.

And yes, I know Jesus was a Jew, but frankly, I have a hard time grasping that concept altogether. First of all, he could not have had a more gentile name. I mean, come on, Jesus Christ! But of course, one of my relatives would have been like, "Oh, I heard he shortened it, anglicized it. Yeah, it was originally Christowitz."

Another reason I don't buy Jesus as a Jew? He was a carpenter. Come on, our people are not known for their work with their hands. But again, my aunt Eleanor would have been like, "Oh, he owned the entire construction company. No, he wasn't out in the field! He was in the office with the books."

I don't know—maybe Chanukah is better left as is. It's worked for a number of years without our messing with it. It's one of the first recorded stories of conservation, which is rather cool. I guess it's easy to get caught up in our nothingness during the holiday season, but ultimately, Chanukah is a pretty nifty story about our survival in a time of great strife. We are a strong and determined people. And a happy people. Yes, happy. (Although our PR firm never really portrays us that way.)

If I could leave you with one fact about our tribe, it would be this little interesting nugget: Jews have the lowest

incidence of suicide among all religions. Are you as surprised to hear that as I was? I don't know why that is, sta-
tistically. My only hunch would be that in our deepest,
darkest moments there's this small voice that's like, "Oh, my
God, I hate my life! I can't believe it, I don't want to go on!"
Then, after a heavy sigh, hope springs eternal—"Oh, look!
Cake!"

Truman Defeats Dewey!

It was decided. Decided long ago. Yes, the definitive decision was, unequivocally, children were not for us.

It's okay to devote yourself to yourselves if it's a "processed" decision. And it was. Therapist approved. We were good to go.

So while those poor saps crouched down when Little Whoever threw his sippy cup from his high chair for the millionth time, we were vacationing at the Punta Mita Four Seasons in sunny Meh-hi-co, having a couples massage by two dark-eyed beauties outside in the balmy breeze. Wish you were here!

And then, something happened. Stirrings at first. A hypothetical thrown out to the loved one on a shared errand to the dry cleaners. Followed by an "I'm just spitballing here" type of conversation on a too long car ride. "We're just talking about it. No one's doing anything. I know it's crazy, but what if we *did* have a baby?" And pretty soon, the definitive decision's officially on the bubble. And then the next thing you know, everything's just gone kablooey.

Yes, sometimes the best laid plans stage a coup. And very late in the middle of the night, it finally becomes official. The pollsters were indeed wrong. You can toss all the newspapers saying Mr. Dewey won the election, people, because Truman just kicked Dewey's ass.

How did this mutiny come about? Blame it on the appearance of one character who seems to be the perennial uninvited guest lately—Mr. Big Picture. Yes, Mr. Big Picture sashays in with his Robert Wagner hair, perfectly white chompers, and takes center stage.

"I'm not up for this today, Big Picture. I don't like you. You're big and scary and you're a drag. You'll probably bring up Sartre and make me worry if I'm pronouncing him correctly. Frankly, I much prefer your little brother, Little Picture. I like how he rolls. All in the moment, here and now. The fun brother. Where's he?"

Big Picture suddenly gets sad and pensive and says, "Little Picture's in recovery at Promises in Malibu, dealing with his alcohol and substance abuse problems. Intimacy issues, too."

"Oh, bummer. Tell him I say hi!"

Big Picture gets on with it. He's a yakker and he wants answers. "I just stopped by because I got a question for ya. Got a Corona?"

"Yeah, but that's not the question, is it?"

"No. I'm just a little parched." I get him his beer. "Thanks. So, little lady. Whatcha gonna leave behind here when you're gone?"

"That's a pretty bold question right out of the box."

"I'm Big Picture, toots. That's pretty much my *only* question."

"Well, if you must know, I'm going to leave behind a rather extensive body of work in comedy, of which I am quite proud."

"Work doesn't count. Unless you're Einstein. Or Oprah."

"All right, we're thinking about having a baby. Probably not going to happen. It's a giant decision."

"Yeah, and so is choosing a wireless plan. Have you seen how long some of those contracts are for?"

"Back to me, Big Picture."

"Like I'd ever forget."

"And don't even get me started on how old the two of us are. I just turned fifty! Do you have any idea what it's like at the stroke of midnight and AARP tracks you down like a wanted felon?"

"Yes, I'm on their board."

"Look, I'm just too old to start having kids."

"Men your age do it all the time without a second thought." Ouch! Big Picture just Eve Ensler–ed the feminist!

"And the bottom line is, I'm too into myself, way too selfish to have a baby."

"Selfish people have kids all the time. You think they

found Paris Hilton in one of the laundry chutes in their hotels? Come on, get over yourself. You've got seven rescue dogs at home. What do you call taking care of them?"

"Oh, having a child is *way* different."

"Not all that much, doll."

"But Big Pic—and I'll whisper this one—what if I regret it?"

"You won't. You're just being a pussy. *Love!* Aren't you getting it yet, lady? 'Shine on us all, set us free/Love is the answer'!"

"Isn't that from an England Dan and John Ford Coley song from the seventies?"

"Yeah, but Todd Rundgren wrote it, so I don't feel like a hack quoting it. Look, sweetheart, you know all this stuff. You're just making me say it so you'll really believe it. Typical of the self-involved. Can I go now?"

Big Picture splits, and suddenly you're staring at your former self from the other side. Remember when Scooby-Doo would cock his head and go "Errrrr?" That's exactly what happened. But I'm used to "Errrr?" I fell in love with a woman for the first time at forty. That's a helluva "Errrr?" So the itinerary changed. We would become parents.

We decided to adopt. My having a kid would have been a science experiment at this point, and Lori having it—well, the thought of some vagabond stranger's seed growing deep inside the woman I infinitely love was just plain unimaginable to me. And once you've adopted animals and seen what a mitzvah that is, adopting a person does seem to be the next logical step.

We settled on adopting a Hispanic baby and brought home our boy at ten months old. Our boy, Bruno. Bruno, that was his name when we adopted him, and we kept it. Nothing worse than a brown-skinned boy running around named Tyler. His first word was "agua." Maybe because of the time he spends with his nanny, Lucita—but we prefer to think of it as a shout-out to his Latino peeps. His second word? "Da Da." Yep, we're batting a thousand!

And the fun thing is, now that we've infiltrated the former enemy's camp, you learn some of their secrets. Like that when they sleep, you sleep. Like that expensive toys are ridiculous to buy when a Tupperware container blows them all away. That you should never let your baby play with your TV remote unless you're okay with a hundred-dollar service call afterward.

And the self? Good news to report on that front. See, it turns out that having a kid is narcissist heaven because your kid is your reflection. His brilliance is recycled *us*. So it's channeled a bit differently, but the ego still gets some good cardio going.

And yes, it's demanding. But so is Pilates. And yes, it takes patience, but so does the Saturday *New York Times* crossword puzzle. But let me tell you something—when it's *your* baby and he throws his sippy cup down from his high chair for the millionth time? It's still not adorable. But putting your baby to sleep by simply rocking them in your arms? Outrageous. Delicious. And what about that baby smell that comes out from the top of their heads? Sweet Jesus, if we could somehow bottle it and make bad people smell it, I swear there would be a lot less evil in this crazy world.

Sure, we still torture ourselves sometimes with the math game—when he's bar mitzvahed, we'll be this age. When he graduates high school, we'll be bladdity blunk. But we're getting close to stopping that. It really serves no purpose other than to get freaked out hearing the year *2024*.

So I wish I could tell you we should have done this sooner, but I think I'd be lying. Ironically, forty-three and fifty seem to have been the perfect ages for us to become parents. Why didn't this revelation happen twenty years ago? I have no idea. But that's the first thing I'm going to ask when I pick up Little Picture at rehab. He needs a ride. He'll refresh my memory.

Take Five, Japan

Technology and I have an uneasy truce. We both respect each other's right to be here but would prefer to have nothing to do with each other, if at all possible.

There are people who actually look forward to finding out the launch date of the next thing Apple is coming out with, while I, on the other hand, am overwhelmed by anything that involves a cord. *My* nirvana would be if nothing new ever came out again. Say hello to the original gangsta Luddite! Yes, life isn't easy when you're a landline-lovin', day-planner-usin', longhand-writin' gal like me.

There are plenty of reasons for my lack of aptitude in the techno world. The first being, I was born with the curse of being mono-focused. I can only do one thing at a time. Otherwise I feel completely overwhelmed. Walking and chewing gum at the same time? A joke to some, but a real challenge to others.

For example, like *nobody* in L.A., I can't drive and talk on my cell phone at the same time. I can't. Even with a hands-free device for the car, it's still a complete failure. A friend reminded me of this when I abruptly ended our recent call by saying, "I gotta call you back. I'm making a right on Wilshire." And I know, not talking in the car does guarantee that I don't get a lot accomplished during the day. But I'm a writer, so I'm not really supposed to.

Learning a cell phone—putting the numbers in, familiarizing myself with the features—it's all too much for a person like me. (So is getting a letter mailed, but that's another story.)

When I think about it, I was probably happiest phone-wise in 1973. It was all so simple then. The phone rang, you answered it and talked. There wasn't the luxury of caller ID. If someone called that you didn't want to speak to, you actually had to get creative. And back then, if you tried somebody and they weren't there? "Oh, well. Guess I'll have to catch them another time." Simple. I like that.

In the eighties, I did stand-up on a lot of cruise ships, and I always remember telling people before I left, "I'll be unreachable." And I was. Because twenty years ago, if you got a phone call on a cruise ship, it meant only one thing. Guaranteed: Somebody croaked. (Ironic, because in today's techno world, the only time you are truly unreachable is when *you* die.)

"Unreachable." I miss that. Because I do think there still

is big value in "unreachable." Everyone doesn't have to be involved in all of our experiences. But technology makes us feel, makes us need, that they should be.

Like a friend of mine called last week while away on vacation. "Dude! I'm in Africa on a safari! Right now I'm looking at a fucking lion and talking to you."

And I was thinking, *Well, you can always talk to me. But looking at a lion? Is it so bad to immerse yourself completely in that rare lion moment? Soak that up 100 percent?* (And then I was also thinking, *Maybe my buddy's "looking" at the lion should be upgraded to "monitoring" the lion, so that he makes sure that he's coming home. With his torso.*)

"One thing at a time": It's a serious mantra for yours truly. And I take it to some wacky extremes. Like at home when I eat my one coveted dessert of the day, I ask that my partner, Lori, not talk to me while I'm devouring said dessert. I find that words distract me from my caloric reverie. And she has been very gracious in accommodating my lunacy. Once she hears the stirrings of that peanut clusters bag, she knows it's Shhhh! time. All I can say is, "Thank you, God, for sending someone to love me."

And yet I remain ever open-minded to technology. I even gave the robots of the techno world a shot and enlisted their help. But they too abandoned me.

We had a Range Rover a while back, and when we got it, the salesman assured us that their GPS was a wonder and a no-brainer for someone "challenged" like me. Personal directions through a speaker in the car? Well, golly! The directions robot even spoke with a British accent.

"Would you be so kind as to make a right at the approaching corner?"

How cool, how cheeky! Until the day when the robot tried to kill us. We were driving along in the carpool lane when he piped up:

"At the next junction, I would urge you to make a left. You might want to consider doing this in approximately one hundred yards."

"Make a left into the guardrail on the freeway? Is that what you'd like, chap? Well, *you* might want to consider cutting back on the Pimm's out there in cyberspace, you homicidal Hugh Grant wannabe."

My fear of technology is so overwhelming that I'm still that idiot who won't fix something online and prefers calling the 800 number and talking to a real-life person for help, even if they are over in someplace like India. Oh, the hours I've logged chatting with our curry-lovin' friends on the other side of the world. And the odd thing is, in the quiet moments during our encounters, most recently about changing my window seat to an aisle on my next United flight, I like to get chatty.

"So how's the weather over there in India today?"

But they never cop to being in a foreign land.

"What? What do you mean, ma'am?"

"Look, Denny, your English is excellent, flawless really. But I know you're speaking to me from India."

"Um, how does seat number 2B sound to you?"

And it's especially frustrating because I want to delve further into our little chat. Stuff like "Did the airline really have to take one of my favorite Gershwin tunes and make it its theme song? I can't hear 'Rhapsody in Blue' anymore without wanting to put my tray table in its upright and locked position." And "So why did you pick the name Denny to be your American one? Shot in the dark: Is your office in India near a Denny's restaurant? Little FYI, just because we Americans name our restaurants something, doesn't mean they're the most popular names. Now let me speak to your supervisor, Long John Silver."

So it's safe to say at this point that I don't like or welcome change. "I Am What I Am" was not just a lame gay song from *La Cage Aux Folles*. And the beauty of my age is, I don't have to change. Ten, twenty years ago there was a shot there, but now the CLOSED sign is permanently affixed to the door of my head. And what still astounds me is, the people who are into these gadgets, the vast majority of my friends and people I know, won't stop trying to convert me. And here is their tried and true fallback line:

"But it's so easy!"

I always want to add two words to the end of that sentence. ". . . *for you*! So easy *for you*!"

They mean well, but they're really the technology world's Jehovah's Witnesses.

"I'm glad it works for you, I am. You seem happy and at peace now that you have a new PDA and Bluetooth, and sure, you can leave some literature. But I still ain't joining your little group today."

Or they say, "Wait a minute—you still use a *film* camera? Omigod, you should use a digital. You can erase the pictures while they're still in the camera."

"But I don't wanna erase the pictures while they're still in the camera. I wanna get the pictures back from the weird lady at the photo place, look through them, and then toss the ones I don't like into my garbage can."

"You still listen to CDs? Are you kidding? If you had an iPod, you could store six thousand songs."

"Six thousand songs? Just hearing that number makes me tense. I don't need that pressure. I just wanted to hear 'Sweet Baby James' on the ride home from the dentist while I was coming off the nitrous."

"But you can still listen to James Taylor with an iPod—plus you'll have room for another five thousand nine hundred ninety-nine songs."

"Really? I don't think Time Life has that many songs."

The saddest day was when I realized that even my beloved TV had abandoned me and joined the innovation parade. When exactly did a TV set become a TV *system*? Oh, for the days when you took it out of the box, plugged it in, and voilà, *Bewitched*! And this was before VCRs and TiVo, when the only thing you had was your loud voice.

"Hey, come on, you're missing it! Samantha is turning the second Darrin into a toad just before he goes to work for his big presentation!"

And if the *Brady Bunch* started to look a little green, you simply whacked the side of the console with your fist like Dad did. That was about as bad as it could get. But no more. A phalanx of things constantly go wrong now. My heads-up is when I point the remote at the TV and nothing happens. Then I'm out of ammo. And Lori and I just look at each other and think, *Can't one of us be the man now?*

(Do you ever find a remote and you don't know what it goes to? You go around the house like an idiot, pointing it at things to see if anything happens?)

My father came to visit a few years back and asked to watch some TV. I set him up in the guest room, but after a few minutes, I didn't hear anything, so I went back to check on him. (Truth be told, he was also in his eighties. At that age, you always want to hear *something* coming from them, regardless.) I opened the door, and there he sat, lost amid a sea of remotes.

"Carol. Give me something with a button for channel up, channel down. And the same for volume. That's all I want."

And I thought forlornly, *Oh, Daddy. Sweet Daddy. Join the club.*

So, Japan, how 'bout it? Could you do a Jew a favor and take five? A moratorium on developing anything new, maybe even just for a day? Then I could catch up on the stuff I already have. Go ahead—kick back and enjoy some of that terrific sake and tempura you came up with. You deserve it, you do. *Domo arigato.*

Two by Two Starts
with One by One

I was not what one would call an "animal person." That was infinitely clear. I didn't grow up with animals, never had a dog or a pet of any kind, just had no interest in them. An animal was a thing—like a lamp or a chair—to me. Dogs, cats—way too dirty, too smelly and unsanitary for a Purell-lover like myself. And even though my parents told me that as a kid I used to cry at the end credits of every *Lassie* episode when Lassie raised his paw, and the first book that ever moved me to tears was *Charlotte's Web*, that was then and this was now. Sure, maybe years ago I could have *become* an animal person, but I was forty. I was formed. A leopard does not change its spots.

But then a monkey wrench was thrown into the equation (and yes, I realize that's the second time I made an animal reference). I fell in love with an animal person named Lori. She had a dog and two cats—a malty-poo named Murphy, and her cats, Max and Dexter. Besides the fact that, after a life of dating and marrying men, this was the first woman I had ever fallen in love with, well, now, didn't I just find myself in quite the quandary? Because how you feel about animals in a relationship is very different from, say, how you feel about falafel. "You like it; I don't. Okay, no prob. So we won't be hitting any Middle Eastern restaurants together."

But animals are part of a much bigger package. And that package included her undying love of these beings who shared her life. Shared it big-time! Things that were my worst nightmare. Like at night, they all slept in bed together. Like when she kissed the dog, the malty-poo, she kissed it right on the mouth. And yup, the Big Kahuna of them all: When in the presence of her animals, the object of my affection cooed and referred to herself with them as "Mommy."

What was a nonanimal person to do? I did what most of my kind probably do—I tolerated it. I didn't get it, that's for sure, and observed it from afar, like watching a PBS special on Jane Goodall with the apes. *I'm just in a different culture with different mores,* I thought. It's like when you go to Italy and they eat the salad course last. Whatever, foreign people. Vive la différence! (I've been to France, too.)

Oh, sure, Lori tried to get me to actually engage with the animals, but I would have nothing to do with it. In fact, when we first got together, I was working twelve-hour days, writing and producing for a new sitcom. And when a show doesn't have its legs yet, it's incredibly stressful. I would go to Lori's place, inconsolable at the end of these horribly taxing days, and Lori would look at me and say, "Just pet my dog, Murph. Really, I swear, you'll feel so much better." And I thought she was crazy. I was sort of offended even—offering up a trivial solution to some hard-core stress. "Pet your dog? No, thanks. The only animal I want to fondle right now is some Grey Goose. On the rocks, giant tumbler."

And it worked okay for a while. That is, until we decided to move in together at my place. Then this animal thing really came to a head. But I was not shy and not to be deterred. I said, "I have no interest in living with a dog and two cats. I'm sorry, I love you, but I am what I am. In this house, there will be nothing fur-covered, and that includes your mother in Brentwood."

And this woman who I loved, a person who loved these animals as if she'd actually birthed them, came back to me and said, "I love you, too. And I want to make a life with you. So if you truly cannot live with my animals, so be it. Our dear friend Pat will take the cats, and Murph will live with my folks." And it was at that moment that the sky parted and a bolt of lightning hit me in the head. So hard that I realized, finally, If this woman loves me so much that she'd actually give up these creatures that give her so much joy, what kind of animal am I to deny her them? *What kind of animal am I?*

So we all moved in together and became one ark. And it happened slowly, but it did indeed happen. I think Lori knew somewhere what all animal people know. That is, you cannot *not* love an animal. I dare you. I dare you to live with a dog or a cat for six months and afterward not be as giddy and smitten as a doe-eyed schoolgirl. Their arsenal is too overwhelming; you must surrender.

There were so many things that I didn't know about them when I thought of them as things. Like that they each have an incredibly unique and quirky personality? Sometimes more interesting, complex, and funny than many people I know. Well, that certainly wasn't in the brochure! The pureness and goodness of their souls? Like, a dog won't get you involved in a bad land deal. Or a cat won't compliment you at a party on how fantastic you look, then snipe about you behind your back that you really look like you've "put on a few." And what about that fierce and absolute unconditional love? How do you live without that once you get a taste? Your mere presence walking in the door lighting up their life so instantly, with that metronome of a tail wag? I confess, sometimes I leave my house and come back in a different door just to get another quick fix.

And all they've taught me. I think the not talking—that blows my mind the most about animals. Look, I'm a writer and a Jew. So words and talking are high priorities for me, and animals rely on neither. Oh, sure, they make a loud noise when they have to, but if you have an animal, lemme ask you something. Have you ever not known what he or she is feeling, with just a slight head cock, a sigh, a certain look in their eyes? It took animals to show me that we humans talk way too much.

I've even learned more about men, having male dogs. Like a male dog will lift his leg and mark even when he doesn't have to pee. How often does that happen around the office, ladies? So I've learned to take things less personally. That's easy to do when you realize so much behavior is just purely animal-based.

But before you think this transition was completely seamless, think again. The four-legged ones don't make it easy. Oh, no, they don't. Let me tell you, before these animals, I had rugs. Beautiful rugs from the far reaches of the earth, handwoven pieces of art that soon became the animals' high-priced pee pads. See, they prefer not to relieve themselves on things so bourgeois as from the pet supply store. No, they have much better taste than that! And you can't fool them. Replace the pricey stuff with some shmata rug from IKEA, and they will have nothing to do with it. It's like they're saying, "I won't crap on crap, sweetheart. My ass needs something thick and cushy. And preferably from someplace high-end."

So here I am all these years later, the complete convert. I am born again and address you now as an avowed animal lover and protector. Turns out my girl had it right all along and graced me with the greatest gift ever—the key to my better self. We are mommies (Yes, mommies! Who *else* are we to them?) to seven dogs now, all rescues, and I swear if Lori would let me adopt more, we'd do it. I have even looked into buying a custom bed, because a king mattress does not comfortably accommodate two humans plus many dogs.

Sadly, we lost Lori's original two kitties, Max and Dex, a few years ago, along with Murphy, the dog who resurrected me. Man, we look at pictures of them and bawl our eyes out. There's no animal like your first. Ever.

And this is what I love best about life: when it throws you a curveball and you're not even out on the field. Life shows up and says, "You thought you were this kind of person, but guess what? Turns out you're not! Change is possible. Growth is possible. You are so much more than you think."

Loving animals has changed my life. I am truly transformed. I am so much softer, so much fuller than the person that I spoke about at the beginning of this piece. The parts of my heart that were filled with brush have been cleared away. And I think this softness was always there lying dormant inside me, as evidenced by that gush of feelings as a child toward Lassie and *Charlotte's Web,* but that precious metal just needed to be deeply mined.

A leopard can't change its spots? Oh, I beg to differ. Not only can it change its spots, but right before your very eyes, the leopard can morph into a delightful little kitty. You can become the person you never thought you'd be. (And that works both ways, people. You can also become a real prick if you're not careful.) A life without animals, *my* life without loving animals, is unimaginable to me now. It's like living without air, without music.

And when I come home now after a particularly hard day, nothing is better than smushing my face into those coats, those intoxicating seven coats, and I breathe in deeply, and I melt, and dammit, I do feel so much better. Take that, $150-an-hour therapy! Take that! Rugs are so not important, and words are so overrated.

Shhh! I'm Driving

Dear Fellow Motorists,

Hi. I know we don't speak all that often. Oh, sure, we've traded our share of honks and angry hand gestures, but that's par for the course living in L.A., right?

But here's something I've wanted to share for a long time—

I believe that your car is a mode of transportation, not an "opinion pod." I believe that a vehicle is for getting from point A to point B—not for *making* point A and point B. I believe your car is not your blog. In short, your car is not a vehicle, if you will, for us to get to know one another better. So I'm asking for an end to all bumper stickers. I'd pose it as a safety issue, just one more distraction on the road, but I'd be fibbing.

The truth is, I'm just looking for a little peace and quiet out on the open road. Plain and simple, I'm not interested in hearing other people's feelings while I'm driving. (Especially on the ride over to my shrink's. You're distracting me from *me*.) I feel that your car is not a place to share your political leanings, your life philosophies or band preferences.

And certainly most of all, not for sharing your children's scholastic achievements. Those kinds of back-end proclamations really stick in my craw. I just don't really care that your kid Ashley is an honor student at Oakdale Elementary. In fact, I've lived very happily up to this point being out of the loop with all things Oakdale. Although, hearing about your children's failures? Well, frankly, I'm licking my chops at the prospect of that one. May I propose, on the left side of the bumper perhaps, MY DAUGHTER MEAGAN IS AN ABJECT FAILURE AND PERSONAL DISAPPOINTMENT AT OAKDALE ELEMENTARY. Followed by, on the right side of the bumper, AND SHE AIN'T ALL THAT CUTE, EITHER. MY HUSBAND'S GENES . . . WHAT CAN YOU DO? That would bring a smile to my face faster than any accomplishment short of world peace.

In particular, let me take to task a few specific bumper stickers:

1. For the love of God, man, would you finally take off that KERRY/EDWARDS '04 sticker? Talk about not moving on! No wonder you won't make the

right on red when it's completely clear. (And if you tell me there's a GORE/LIEBERMAN sticker underneath that one, I might just have to take you apart.)

2. I'D RATHER BE FISHING. Here's a concept! Make the left instead of a right at this corner and head straight. It leads to a little place called "the ocean."

3. WATCH OUT! I'M ETHAN'S GRANDMA! What I wouldn't give to pass this old biddy with *my* bumper sticker—NO, *YOU* WATCH OUT, GRANNY. I'M ETHAN'S CRACK HO IN A REAL BAD MOOD.

4. THERE IS NO EXCUSE FOR DOMESTIC VIOLENCE. Amen to that, my brutha. But then why are you riding the ass of the car in front of you, like your wife who doesn't listen? Your sensitive man exterior does not jive with the aggressive tailgating tool. Sync up, dude!

5. WHAT WOULD JESUS DO? Well, when stuck behind someone crawling at ten miles an hour, my answer would be, "Jesus would gun it, lard ass!"

6. I'M PROUD OF MY CUB SCOUT. I'm at a loss with this one. It's simply got no heft. It's about as hard-hitting as the declaration "I like lettuce and tomato sandwiches." The only rationale for a bumper sticker like this is if the driver had been accused of *not* being proud of his Cub Scout. Like, the den got together and suddenly turned on him. "Don? How

do we say this? . . . At the last jamboree, we noticed your enthusiasm for your Cub Scout to be rather lackluster. When he displayed his prize knots, did you really mean to say, 'Okay, what else you got?' And capturing the fort is a big deal, Don. Let your son be aware of that!"

So let's start peeling, America. Not peeling out, but off. Let that naked bumper shine like the day your uncle Moe gave you his old Dodge Dart. And please reserve your thoughts and feelings for the stationary landlocked.

All my best,

Carol in the Car Behind You

Fighting for Your Fake Tits

I love being politically active. Especially when it's from the comfort of my Relax the Back desk chair at home. How nice to help out a just cause with simply a click of a mouse at my computer. I'm changing the world and not irritating my irascible lumbar area at the same time!

So I got this email the other day from the fine folks over at NOW, the National Organization for Women, urgently requesting my help. They asked me, as a card-carrying feminist, to write my congressman and ask for better-quality breast implants. Seems that the FDA is quite lax in this department and not too big on demanding evidence of silicone's long-term safety.

But as I readied up my mouse to give the requisite click of support, I took pause. And I thought about how I was lending my support to something that I would never person-ally consider doing. Besides the fact that nature made sure that this would never be a personal issue, it's something that I'm really against (except, of course, for reconstructive sur-gery). I think women alter their bodies way too much these days. And I'm pretty positive most of the vixens down at NOW are with me on this one. Breast implants are for *them, those* women, not us. (Ironic, because if the implant seekers are looking for help with this issue, they're damn well sure not surfing the NOW website.) And so I thought, *Why am I fighting for your fake tits when you're not bringing anything to my party?*

This brought to mind a larger concern for me—I'm hav-ing some problems with women today. Some younger women in particular. And I know that's not all "sisterly" and Gloria Steinem–like and "NOW" of me to say, but it's how I feel.

Sure, I know that you have to be extra careful at my age when you criticize younger women, because you want to make sure that it's not just misplaced anger about envying their youth. But believe me, I don't envy their youth. I envy their *diet,* that's for damn sure. When I think about the sheer volume of food I was able to eat when I was twenty-three—an endless parade of club sandwiches, onion rings, hot fudge sundaes—and then the next day, "Hi, skimpy bikini!" Yeah, *that* I miss.

So what's my beef exactly? I'll share. It seems as though a lot of younger women today think that the women's move-ment is over. ("Women! Yay! We did it! Mission accom-plished! Hey, thanks for all the strides you made and all the rights you ensured, but I got a cardio yoga class to get to!") It's like we handed them the torch and they promptly blew it out. ("'Cause this thing's kinda heavy and hurting my arm and I got a mannie-peddie appointment at three. I swear, my hands and feet look like a gibbon's!")

Let's face it, feminism just isn't cool anymore. My friend has a daughter who currently goes to Vassar, and in a women's studies class the professor asked how many students in the room would call themselves feminists—and three students raised their hands. At *Vassar*. (And one of them was a guy. At *Vassar*.)

But if the prof had asked, "How many of you think that women should have all the same rights men do? And be equally paid? Plus have control over their own reproductive lives?" I'll bet you everybody would have raised their hands.

So something's seriously off.

People hear the word "feminist" and they immediately think of angry, hairy-underarmed, Birkenstock-wearin' lesbians. (Okay, so maybe I'm two out of four, but that doesn't change the fact that the word "feminist" is broken.) And it's unfortunate, because the pledge drive needs new faces now more than ever—because there's a whole lotta trouble going down, my friends.

And I worry that it's going to reach crisis levels soon. Because any movement needs the next generation engaged, or everything goes haywire. Like there isn't enough madness already going on in our little part of the world, but outside it's reached insane proportions: Girls as young as seven in India are forced into prostitution. A Russian woman answers an ad to be a nanny and is kidnapped by sex traffickers. There's a video on YouTube of an Iraqi teenage girl getting stoned to death for loving a boy of the wrong religion. *Stoned to death* for something that's a plot point in our musicals.

And I know, it's all so heavy and depressing and you'd much rather be watching the YouTube video of the bunny dressed like Charo doing the cha-cha. But if you don't think that Iraqi girl is connected to you, you're wrong. She's tied to me and you (or a woman you love, if you're a man) and every XX chromosome out there, because we're all members already of a little group called the Vagina Club. Look down, and if you got one, you're in! (We'll even take you, too, trannies.) And if I know one thing about the survival of a species, it's this—you gotta take care of your own, or else, who will?

Because, the Phil Donahues and Alan Aldas notwithstanding (geez, even the references for male feminists are twenty years old), men are never gonna step up like we want them to. Plain and simple, not their issue. (And let's be honest, how involved are *we* in the fight against prostate cancer?) Oh, believe me, if something goes haywire with Cialis, the menfolk will be rioting in the streets. But we gotta face the fact—we're on our own.

So after this mental pipe burst, did I ultimately click for the better, safer breast implants? Yes. Yes, I did. It is, after all, about women's health, and I'm still all up in that.

Okay, so maybe I clicked this time. But let me tell you something, ladies. I'm tired. Bone-tired. Of clicking, of writing letters, going to fund-raisers, throwing fund-raisers, sending money, lots and lots of money (I do work hard for it, honey) for stuff that affects you, too, bitch.

I march. Oh, I march my ass off. And you know what I've noticed? You ain't there.

Where are you?

You're in Beverly Hills clutching your Chihuahua, patiently lined up out at the True Religion Jeans sale three hours ahead of time so you can get just the right pair you saw on Nicole Richie (who does *what*, by the way?). Or you're standing in line somewhere else, maybe to buy a tote that says I AM NOT A PLASTIC BAG, when I could have told you that.

Meanwhile, back at the march, it's just me and the old broads. Well, listen up, tube-top-wearer. You better put down that Chihuahua (it does occasionally have to pee, you know), root around in that overstuffed closet of yours, find yourself some comfortable shoes (you probably have a pair from last Halloween when you went as a gym teacher), *and get out there with us.*

It's not like I don't enjoy the exercise at all the pro-choice marches. But news flash: Reproductive rights ain't exactly my issue anymore. My baby-making feature is now on "off." I'm happy to report that my ovaries just bought a lovely condo in Boca. So if you don't wish to end your unintended pregnancy in some guy's basement who doesn't even have a doctor's license and his last job was operating the lift at Meineke, you might want to start marching, toots. Like *now.*

'Cause if you think it's over, it's never over. Let me tell

you a little story about my grandma from the Bronx, Jenny Silverman, who I'm pretty sure stayed home most of the day on November 7, 1916. One reason was because she was probably exhausted from clubbing a carp over the head (which had been swimming earlier in the day in her bathtub) so she could make homemade gefilte fish for her precious family. But another reason she was most likely home was because November 7, 1916, was Election Day, and she didn't vote. Not because she didn't care—but because she wasn't allowed.

You see, in those days, they didn't think Grandma's brain as a female was important enough to participate. And in the grand scheme of time, "girlfriend," that's a blip. It's like yesterday—and it could be yesterday again so easily, if you keep shopping and shopping, believing that fashion magazines are bibles and staying so, so damn complacent.

When exactly did Eloise from the Plaza Hotel stop being an over-the-top fictional character and become a real live person? Remember when excess was embarrassing?

Growing up on Long Island, I went to public school with the heir to a large home department store (I can't say which one, but it could rhyme with Hortunoff), and this girl had a chauffeur who occasionally drove her to school. But it made her so uncomfortable that she had him drop her off a block away. Today, not only would that girl be busting at the seams to be squired in that limo, but her friends would be salivating on the sidelines. 'Tis a different world.

You've come a long way, baby. Yes, you sure have. But

the idea wasn't to get there and then open up a folding chair. As much as it interferes with your go-go lifestyle, you've got to think about the long line behind you. You've got to care about the less fortunate—and I don't mean salesgirls. And you've got to vote for people who pay attention to this stuff.

We can be so much more. So much more than Jimmy Choo–seeking shopping bots. So much more than competitive "Who Wore It Best?" scorekeepers. So much more than überconsuming "Real Housewives." We're mothers; we birth the entire world. So can't we put a little of that mothering instinct toward one another?

And if you young'uns say you don't have time to participate, well, then, okay, but you should really give some money. There are plenty of people out there who'll get the sweat stains that you don't want, but I guarantee you they're underfunded. If every woman out there who has the means gave just 1 percent of her income to any group fighting to erase these injustices, do you know what kind of difference that would make in the world? (And please don't pull the recession card when I know what you spend on a weekly basis at Starbucks.)

So jump on in, ladies. It's never too late. I know you'd like to think differently, but the road ahead? It's still unpaved. Oh, I'm happy to stand up for your vagina. I am. But frankly, mine's tired and would enjoy a nice cup of tea right about now.

And you know what else? Screw implants. I bet your tits are just fine. I'd love them and leave them alone if I were you.

Holiday Gift Guide

We pretend the holiday season is about sharing, family, togetherness, blah, blah, blah. But "What did you get?" pretty much sums it all up. That's what your coworkers are gonna ask January second when you park your suddenly larger ass back in its cubicle. Not "How did you and your loved ones get closer this holiday? Mine? We rescued a pig off a truck headed for the Oscar Mayer factory. He's living with Nana now, even though he's not kosher."

Come on, who are we kidding? The jig is up.

They say, "It's the thought that counts." What they don't say is, "they" are cheap people. You know who I'm talking about. The same people who when the check comes at an expensive restaurant suddenly seem to be wearing a straitjacket. Not even the pretend move for the wallet. They always go, "Hey, I'll get the next one," and the next one's always at IHOP. "Don't look a gift horse in the mouth?" Sorry! I'm prying Flicka's choppers so wide open I can fit my entire head inside.

So no surprise, then. I'm pretty straightforward in my feelings about gift-giving, and basically it's a simple philosophy—quid pro quo. Tit for tat. What I'm putting out, I want to see coming back. Like, if I buy you an eight-quart silver-plated rolltop chafing dish, I'm not going to fully appreciate the gag gift of a talking George Bush doll who, when you pull his finger, says, "Hey, Saddam, here's a weapon of mass destruction!" and then farts. Amusing? You bet. But it's around these times that I'm sorry I didn't get *you* a gag gift as well. Like the eight-quart silver-plated rolltop chafing dish with the exploding top. That might get a laugh, too. And a lawsuit. But it was funny, right? (And as a side note, by the way, must it be called a "chafing" dish? Who can we speak to about that? I always feel like a chafing dish should be pretreated with Vaseline before a party so it won't be so cranky.)

Why am I so hard-boiled about this gift business? Well, there's a genetic marker, meaning I grew up among Jews. My father? King of tit for tat. Years ago when I got married, my parents threw me and my eventual ex our wedding. And when I asked if there was anything I could do to help, my father replied, "Yeah. You can make a list of what all the guests give you," most of them being my parents' friends. And make a list I did. And guess who checked it twice? Afterward, my father read it as a vindication or an indictment of each person he knew. "Let's see. Next door neighbor Ernie Pinter. Two hundred dollars! *That man* is a class act. *That man*—a real gentleman. I must remember to buy him a pound cake the next time I'm at the bakery. Lou Kastenbaum. What? Twenty-five bucks? The place setting cost twenty-five bucks! I gave his Leonore a C-note for her bat mitzvah. And the wife still has a casserole dish she never returned, right, hon? All right, who else . . ."

Then there's another piece of family history that I should add. My family suffered from a common affliction among my people called "genericitis." Sound familiar? For example—feel like having a nice cold glass of orange juice? Some refreshing *Tropicana* orange juice, maybe? Well, go down the block, because here at Shtetl Leifer, we got frozen A&P orange juice. And as my father was quite fond of saying, "It's a quarter of the price and it's the same thing." No, it's not the same thing. It's a glob of orange goo you mix with tap water that quickly becomes clumps of orange goo that refuse to have anything to do with said tap water. "People say they don't even taste the difference." These "people," dear "Papa, can you hear me," had their taste buds surgically removed.

Another example of the cost-cutting madness? *TV Guide.* Wasn't allowed chez Leifer. Why? Because the TV listings were free in the newspaper. "So why buy a newspaper?" I foolishly asked. Not a question taken seriously in a Jewish home. Calling information when there's a phone book in the closet? It was akin to ordering a bottle of Dom Pérignon in a restaurant and then not drinking it.

This all came to an unfortunate head when as a seven-year-old child I had some dental surgery. Some procedure worthy of the promise of a gift afterward. And when my parents asked what I wanted, I did not waver. Did not waver, like a mighty oak. I wanted a Chatty Cathy. Chatty Cathy, the A-list doll who other dolls bowed down to. Pull her string and this bitch talked. And not just talked, went on and on. *So* up my Jew alley! Again, Chatty Cathy. I was very clear. But sure enough, still groggy from the kiddie anesthesia wearing off, there she was, placed into my very own arms: *Babblin' Barbara*—the knockoff version of Chatty Cathy.

Babblin' Barbara—ugh, what a train wreck this chick was. Reeking of cheap Taiwanese sweatshop child-labor plastic. Not pretty *at all*. In fact, she had a somewhat haunting look of abject fear across her face, like she was staring into an open hand. Her wink mechanism was completely off in one eye. You had to viscerally shake her like an abusive babysitter to get it going right. And most important, her "talkin' string" was constantly getting clogged in her back. You didn't want to play with her as much as rush her to the emergency room and get her some counseling. Thanks a lot, Leifers! My father, sensing my disappointment, obliviously offered once again his now-famous catchphrase. "Carol, Babblin' Barbara is just as good as that high-priced Chatty Cathy." "No, she's not. Babblin' Barbara is a speech-impaired whore!"

This was followed about a year later by another bizarre gift-giving incident, this time having to do with my grandma. For Chanukah, my grandma Becky got me some slippers. And they looked nice enough, even though Grandma admitted that she'd purchased them at a joint called John's Bargain Store. But upon closer inspection of the footwear, I saw that they were *two left slippers.* When I brought this to my grandma's attention, she replied, "Oh, big deal! Believe me, Carol, your foot will conform." This became a source of amusement for my family for many years to come, this two left slippers story. A source of amusement, and confirmation that—if I hadn't known it before—my family was rife with tight nut jobs.

So "What did you get me?" is a pretty loaded question now for yours truly, as you can see. It's obviously fraught with some "old drama," let's call it. And I have discovered that I might just do better getting out of this whole holiday present thing. A gift deserter, if you will. Hightail it up to Canada for the holiday season.

Or maybe I should just change my focus. Once and for all, get out of this vicious cycle of the equalizing scales thing. I don't know—maybe I should rescue a pig. And maybe you'll do it with me. And that will be our gift to each other—the gift of pig liberation. It would be good for our souls. And for the pig. I have read that they're not treated very well, you know. Yeah, that would be good for us. So . . . you wanna drive? Maybe I should, since you did the last time. But I got lunch last time, so maybe it's your turn?

76 Trombones

"The number is seventy-six, Carol. Like the song 'Seventy-six Trombones' from *The Music Man*? If you're ever lost, just remember that. That will get you home." And that's how my father, Seymour, taught me as a kid to remember my home address. My home in my hometown.

I was born at that house on 76 Trombones, otherwise known as 76 Bengeyfield Drive. My older brother and sister were both born in the Bronx, so I have a particular affinity for this spot in East Williston, Long Island. And my mother, Anna, still lives and practices psychology there, at the age of—hold on to your hats—eighty-eight.

See, I disagree, Mr. Burt Bacharach. I believe a house *is* a home. How could it not be when it's the only home you've ever known? But recently my mother has had a change of heart about the house. She says that since my dad died, there are too many memories there. So she's put the house on the market, which, to tell you the truth, has thrown me into a tailspin so discombobulating, I can't even begin to plumb its depths. I am so attached to this piece of 2,200 square footage—which, yes, I know now because I went on the real estate site where it's listed, horror of horrors.

When your history is a house's history, there's a bond there. It sorta feels like my twin—except I think that I weathered the seventies a little better. I know every sight, sound, and smell that emanates from its four walls, so much so that I could be on a quiz show and get every answer right.

Like that frightening, absurdly loud banging sound? That's the knocker in the shape of an American eagle on the front door, which, if anyone ever used it to be polite instead of ringing the doorbell, sounded as if the Cossacks were coming for us.

And that dreamy aroma wafting through the screen window into my room in spring? That's a little thing called honeysuckle, but drink it in while you can 'cause it doesn't last long. And that meant that soon I could be getting the hell outta Dodge a lot more on my bike.

And this spot here? This is the rec room, and here's where my parents summoned me down to do this new dance called the Pony for the Buxbaums, who lived next door, and I joyfully obliged.

And over there is where the record player was. And one night my brother, sister, and I cranked the Mamas and the Papas' new album so loud that my father came downstairs, yelled at us, and threatened to take the album away. That is, until he heard the song "Monday, Monday" and suddenly had a religious experience. So much so that he concocted this contraption for the turntable with a piece of string so that he could play "Monday, Monday" over and over again without having to get up and do it by hand. (I have no idea how he constructed it, but my father was very handy that way.)

Now let's proceed outside, shall we? Here? That's where the crocuses come up, even though it's still cold out, right by where the milkman used to leave us milk. Yes, milkman, young people! When I was so small that I couldn't differentiate the lids on the bottles of milk, and I screamed in agony when I happened to take a sip of skim milk.

And I know not just every spot, but every spot in every incarnation that the house has had. Like our rooms, before 1971 and then after, when my aunt Evie, the interior decorator, helped us pick out the latest geometric wallpaper and shag carpeting and got our rooms all groovified. Like the bench in the basement that used to be where we stored our toys, until my father went out in 1982 and bought this new-fangled thing called a VCR, for a *thousand dollars,* and put that on the bench, so he could tape me doing stand-up on TV shows.

I know this house so well, I can actually tell what room someone's in by the sound of that particular door closing. And speaking of door closing, as a teenager, I could adjust my door slam in that house like a finely honed tennis swing to perfectly convey my exact mood to my parents—a light touch for the Janis Ian "I'm hurting, but you'll never understand" door slam, to the full-on Janis Joplin "I can't believe you fascists won't let me wear this tube-top to David Lieber-stein's pool party" door slam.

This is the house I sped eighty miles an hour to get to when I was in college in Binghamton and awoke one morning to find that my face had broken out in forty-seven different zits. My mother promised a speedy appointment with a quality dermatologist. So where *else* do you run when your face has sprouted forty-seven zits?

This house has been my oasis from everything. And no matter how old I've gotten, when that taxi from the airport turns onto Bengeyfield Drive and I repeat the same phrase I've said for the last forty years, "It's the fourth house on the left. Where the white professional sign is," a part of me finally lets go. I'm safe. I'm home.

It is the house where my father passed away. On a Sunday night, while watching *60 Minutes,* just like he always did every Sunday night. In a moment, at the age of eighty-six. That he went that way actually brings me and my family a modicum of joy. Because he loved that house and was so proud of it and its story, which he told with great relish. (And, sometimes, while applying relish to a Hebrew National hot dog.)

How my father in 1952 was all set to buy half of a two-family home in Little Neck, Queens, when his partner from his optical practice on Thirty-fourth Street mentioned a brand-new development going up on Long Island and how my father could, pardon the pun, get in on the ground floor. Sure, it was farther out from the city than Queens, but walking distance to the Long Island Rail Road station. And yeah, it was a lot of money back in those days, but my father had a hunch and always proclaimed, "Damn if you don't gotta trust a hunch!" So he took a chance and put in an offer on this house with the funny street name, Bengeyfield Drive. My father always laughed at how he didn't sleep a wink the night he put in the offer, secretly hoping that the loan wouldn't go through, he was so nervous about making the mortgage payments on this *twenty-thousand-dollar* house. And over the years, he told this story a lot. It meant so much to him that that hunch had turned out to be his best friend. And then as a family, we all imagined the miserable existence we would have had out in Little Neck. "Little Neck. What kind of name is that anyway? . . . Can you pass the peas, please?"

So how can this place not be mine anymore? "Too many memories." I completely respect and get that from the woman who was married to my father for sixty-two years. But while she now wants to distance herself as much as possible from this place, all I want to do is hold it tight and never let it go.

My brother and sister are both emotional about it as well, but not nearly as much as I am. But then, I already have a penchant for holding on to things. Like, I'm a big clutterer. And I've endlessly tried working on it. Once I even took a Learning Annex course called Letting Go of Clutter. And the teacher went through great pains to explain why the class wasn't called Getting Rid of Clutter but was called

Letting Go of Clutter, because de-cluttering is learning how to let go. She took questions at the end, and I raised my hand. "I have a problem that when I travel, I always take the little bottles of shampoo and conditioner home with me, and they wind up cluttering everything. Any advice?" And then the Clutter Lady, who I shall now refer to as the Dalai Lama, told me, "Well, don't take home those little bottles of shampoo and conditioner anymore." Why do the hardest things to learn somehow turn out to be so simple?

So now there's this house sale to contend with, and it's just awful. The thought of other people, strangers, trampling through what I consider sacred ground is overwhelming. And I'm so glad I live three thousand miles away and can't possibly be there for those open houses—I couldn't take it. Those prospective buyers? Their faces—smiling pleasantly at the realtor's schpiel until he turns his back and they grimace at one another as they proceed to trash the next room. It would just destroy me. I even have serious fantasies now about busting up one of these open houses, bursting into the joint swinging a billy club, shouting, "Everyone out! That's right, people. Show's over. And I mean now! Everybody! Yeah, you too, buddy. You're not even seriously interested. You just go to these things 'cause you're lonely. Well, work out your crap somewhere else, Nowhere Man!"

I want it back. I want this house back when it shook like a maraca. When the new coat of Sherwin-Williams paint was drying and the carpet still had tacks so fresh that they nicked your feet. But that's not possible. The truth is, the house is old. Kind of on a respirator, even. The maraca is busted, and all the little beads have spilled out. So here I am—trying to learn again the hardest lesson of life—letting go.

Letting go. Saying goodbye. To me, easily the hardest part of all this. Letting go . . . of the people you love, of the animals that you love as much as you love people, and now letting go of places? Well, isn't that just great? But at least when my father and my animals died, they weren't here any-more to confuse things. But not with a house, kiddies. The house will always be. And with other people inside, making their own "Monday, Monday" stories, creating their own memories. And I will find a way to be okay with that. That's the other thing I've learned about life—you get over it. You do. And not because you want to but because you have to. *You just have to.*

I came across *The Music Man* on cable recently. And I hadn't seen it in quite a while, and I'd forgotten, it's really quite a good musical. That song "Trouble"? The intricate lyrics and how Robert Preston performs it at this insanely syncopated clip? What a nice piece of work. And "Seventy-six Trombones." That song really holds up. It's upbeat, positive, and very jaunty. And when that song filled my ears, I heard it so differently this time. In a way that's really quite hard to describe. Because that song will always tell me, wherever I am, that I am still somewhere very close to being home.

A Dozen Things Men Should Know (but Most Don't)

1. RUNNING WATER IS YOUR FRIEND

Never forget that cologne is for *after* showering, not *instead* of showering. And as far as cologne goes, it's not flea dip, guys. A little drop goes a long way. Believe it or not, you could toss all that manly perfume stuff, anyway—and not just because most guys in cologne commercials look like they have the hots for other guys in cologne commercials. It's because women like the way *you* smell. There's this little thing nature came up with called pheromones that cologne just gets in the way of. So don't mess with animal instinct, and let the "natural you" do its wafting—after, of course, a shower.

2. PONYTAILS

On us? Cute.
On you? Not so cute.

3. YOUR BACK SHOULD NEVER BE MISTAKEN FOR A THROW RUG

If there's a thicket of brush back there, call the fire department to have it cleared, or take it like a man and have it waxed.

4. SKIP THE DUMB QUESTIONS

If your girlfriend is quiet for a while, never ask her, "What are you thinking?" I guarantee the answer won't be "How attractive and unannoying you are" or "The Mets are up seven to six." The same goes for the question "Why aren't you smiling?" That answer will never be fun.

5. DON'T TRUST THE LADIES' ROOM

When you're out somewhere and two women go to the bathroom together, they're definitely talking about you. (Sometimes, I swear, they never even go in the stall, there's so much to discuss.)

6. JUST PUT IT OUT!

A man's breath after a cigar is akin to the odor of a skunk's track shoe after running a marathon. Save the stogies for when you're hanging with your own kind.

7. DON'T GET IT FROM THE RADIO

Taking advice about women from overweight Hawaiian-shirt-wearin' radio shock jocks will get you where they are . . . sitting alone by themselves in a very dark room.

8. IT'S A NUMBERS GAME

If you ask a woman for her phone number but she asks for yours instead, she's not interested in you. In fact, she's more likely to call that 800 number promising a six-figure income buying homes in foreclosure.

9. PULL IT OUT

When the check comes on a first date, if a woman takes out her wallet, it's purely for show. She has no intention of paying, nor should you let her. I know it's not fair, but in exchange you get to run the world.

10. PUT ON YOUR WALKING SHOES

Always walk a woman to her car. Even if it's Gloria Steinem and she declines, walk her to her car. Or in Steinem's case, offer to walk her across the street. (Sorry, Gloria. We're all getting older.) And always wait until a woman's car has driven safely away. (Then you can ask an even bigger man than you to walk *you* to your car.)

11. THE UNFRIENDLY SKIES

Never take your shoes off on a plane. Please find other ways to show your "relaxed side."

12. KEEP IT SHINY

If you're bald, be bald. Women much prefer "no hair" to "dead squirrel hair."

(I'm from New York, and the thirteenth bagel is always free when you order a dozen, so here's an extra added tip.)

13. STAY ON YOUR SIDE

You never need to ask a woman before going on a date if she would like to drive. She never wants to drive. Even if it's Danica Patrick, the answer is no.

The Call of the Sweatpants

What no one tells you about getting older is that you suddenly have a whole new set of priorities. I look back on what I used to crave in my twenties and thirties, and it's all such a hoot now. Drugs? Please. I have no interest in them, unless it's finding something that will finally obliterate my agonizing heartburn after eating just about anything that isn't a staple on an assisted-living menu. Sex? Honestly, after twelve years of sleeping with the same person, it's safe to say there aren't too many somersaults or juggling fire-walkers appearing nightly in our bedroom. Well, once, but it was my birthday and . . . Never mind.

Yes, there's a new obsession in town—comfort. It has become my one true mission. I used to dream as a little girl of one day attending the Academy Awards. And now, all grown-up, I'm proud to say that I've been there five times, either as a writer backstage or as an enthused audience member. And while I'm in the famed Kodak Theatre surrounded by every A-list celebrity imaginable, a pervasive thought running through my mind is, *When the hell can I get out of this sausage casing called pantyhose and these stilts that pose as shoes and back into my favorite sweats and T-shirt?* Sure, talking to Tom Hanks up close and personal is a thrill, but I've had those sweatpants since college. They make cashmere look like scratchy burlap, and being in them is perilously close to a nirvanic experience. I even met Bill Clinton at a fairly intimate dinner party a few years back, and a powerful thought was, *How soon can I get this underwire bra off?* (And possibly the ex-president was thinking just the same thing.)

Comfort. I crave it like a wild-eyed banshee. And the ringleader of its pursuit is definitely my ass. Ooh, and she's a harsh mistress, my friends. See, at this age, the ass doesn't much like being out and about. No, not her scene. She just wants one thing—to be seated as much as possible. And the lady's relentless. Whatever room I walk into, it's just a matter of seconds before I'm casing the joint, searching for a place for the precious keister to park it. An innocent trip to the mall quickly becomes a scouting expedition for where the bratty buttocks are gonna lay low.

Yes, I have become my own ass's bitch. It barks the orders; I merely obey. And being a Jew doesn't help, either. We Jews are fiends for a good seat. (And while you're at it, a spot away from a draft, too, please.)

One purchase created the ass monster. I trace it back to the day when we bought a Barcalounger. Yes, a Barcalounger. Initially for the bargain basement price at a remote Macy's furniture outlet, and the obvious kitsch value. But once it landed in our home, my junk-in-the-trunk took a shining to this piece of furniture like nothing else I've seen. (Oh, the irony! My all-purpose go-to comedy reference for old, fat white men suddenly became my sitting preference of choice.) From watching all my TiVoed shows to doing *The New York Times* crossword puzzle from a sitting-up or reclined position (my call!), everything became such a stone-cold pleasure.

But again, here's where the problem arose. Once enmeshed in said Barcalounger, I was not to be pried out. The idea of getting up seemed positively barbaric. Like it suddenly became a real toss-up if I had to pee real bad. The natural impulse to empty a bursting bladder was no match for America's finest recliner since 1940. Or if I developed a splitting headache while in the lush lap of Mr. B, a tiff soon erupted between the three-foot walk to the bottle of Tylenol and some rich assy goodness down in Barcaville. What kind of power did this slab of American-made foam have over me?

I knew it had gotten to epic proportions when a friend and I recently settled down for a viewing of *Ratatouille* along with her eight-year-old daughter. When the idea of popcorn arose, I had become so engrossed, mind and ass, that I actually offered the small child five bucks to go microwave us up a batch.

The pursuit of comfort has become a monkey on my

back (and all the *more* reason to sit down now, what with the chimp on board!), and I will not be deterred from it. For example, I have been ripped off countless times by valet parkers. I'll drive off at the end of an evening only to find loose change or a sweet pair of sunglasses missing. But sure enough, the next time I pull up to a restaurant and I'm given a choice, what's a little petty theft compared to having to walk three blocks?

Oh, sure, I used to stay for the third encore of a Bruce Springsteen concert. But now my "hungry heart" for beating the traffic is so fierce that the Boss is lucky if this employee stays barely after intermission.

My only consolation in all this is the realization that I am far from alone. We have become an entire society of lazy-ass weenies. Have you noticed the recent accommodations provided to us for the challenges of our daily lives? Ballpoint pens and toothbrushes now come with "comfort grips"? Was there a strain involved with these objects that I had not been privy to before? "Ow! I just wrote a letter with an unsheathed Parker Brothers, and, man, I am feeling it!" Does the toilet really need to flush automatically? I truly feel I had that down, people.

Even a casual encounter at my local shopping center can quickly turn me into a hysterical harpy. Oh, the anger and rage that envelops me when I see that an escalator has the nerve to be broken. "What the *#&% is this? Is it Amish day at the mall? So let me get this straight—I've got to walk up these scary silver spindly steps now to get to *Cinnabon*?"

And when I purchase a new book, I must admit that the first thing I look at is not the author or the subject matter but the heft. This better be some easy reading and not some heavy lifting. Don't think I don't also check the typeface. Anything too textbook-y doesn't stand a chance of making it to the cashier. I haven't been in school for many years and don't plan to be anytime soon.

But I am still a marketer's dream. I will buy anything that promises one iota of added comfort, be it to the ass or any of the nether regions. I recently purchased one of those "Swedish sleep systems" after one too many viewings of their late-night infomercial. Their assurances of mega-comfort were too much for this consumer to take. And looking back, I believe the purchase came down to three specific reasons. One, it was Swedish, and Swedish things seem cool. Number two, it showed a person sleeping peacefully on one side of the mattress while a toddler jumped up and down on the other side. All the while, a glass of red wine sat undisturbed in the middle. "You'll never know your partner is even there!"

Huh, I thought. *My partner, Lori, and I have both wine and a toddler, so we could certainly re-create that at home!*

And the third reason I bought it was their patented "sleep memory system" with the promise that "it molds to your specific body shape and remembers it night after night."

And after we bought this mattress, brought it home, and slept on it, we soon came to realize that—it sucked! My lower back was completely whacked out of shape, and Lori's neck was so bad that she had to find a chiropractor. And looking back, I see that I was the quintessential chump.

First off, the Swedish part? Yeah, Swedish stuff is cool—when it's a thirty-dollar shelf system from IKEA. But in the sleep department? Not as stellar.

And the pitch about not knowing that your partner is there during the night? What was I thinking? I love my partner. I want to know she's there *every* night. Isn't that the point of a relationship? (Turns out, their schpiel is actually a good one for a marriage on the rocks.)

And finally, the "molding to your body" boast? Why did I just blindly buy that fact nugget? Maybe the best thing for a restful night's sleep is for your mattress to completely *obliterate* your body print each night and start over from scratch.

Well, I'd love to go on, but it's late here and the ass is a-callin'. And even though I've been writing this piece in a top-of-the-line Relax the Back office chair, Hiney's tired. Merely sitting just doesn't quite cut it for her now. She wants a bath. Comfort *plus* warm bubbly water. As good a time as any for me to troll through the latest Brookstone catalog. . . . Huh, a hands-free soap dispenser. Motion activated? Add up all that manual strenuous soap-pumping I've been doing over the years, I'm surprised that I haven't developed arthritis. I think I'll circle that. . . .

Dr. Fathead

I have been in therapy almost all of my adult life. My childhood had a lot of gnarly twists and turns that needed untangling, and I've got some funky depressive genes happening on not just one but both sides of my family. And even though I could have purchased a pretty snazzy co-op in Tribeca with all the cash that went to the shrinkage, I firmly believe it's been money well spent. It's especially surprising considering that my first experience with therapy was an all-out disaster.

It all started when I was eleven years old. Around midnight one Sunday evening, I suddenly left my bedroom, walked down two flights of stairs to the den, and took a seat in my father's empty recliner.

"What the hell are you doing down here and not in bed?" my mother asked, quite annoyed, as she was knee-deep in watching *The David Susskind Show* (which, for those of you too young to remember, was only slightly less boring than watching someone read a utility bill).

But I didn't answer, just stared straight ahead like a zombie.

It turned out that I was sleepwalking, and I would not recommend it. One should really save getting up and wandering around in the middle of the night for when you're in your seventies. I was worried and so were my parents. So a plan of action was taken to remedy the situation ASAP by my mother—my mother, the shrink.

Well, I can already hear the collective thought bubbles popping out of your heads. "A shrink? Well, everyone knows that shrinks are the most messed-up parents ever—that is, next to celebrity parents."

And I'm not here to disagree. Because here's the problem with shrinks as parents: They never take their shrink hats off—or maybe it's beards—and replace them with the parent ones. Their worldview is always through the Carl Jung lens, not the Carol Brady lens. They're never mindlessly fluffing up the pillows on a couch—'cause they're beside the couch, listening intently and writing on a legal pad.

And that's exactly what I feel went wrong in the spring of 1968. Because, in true psychologist fashion, my mother decided the best way to remedy the sleepwalking situation was to send me to a Freudian analyst in New York City. There's nothing shrinks love more than calling in more of their own. And not just any analyst in New York City, *her* analyst—the knight in shining armor who'd happied her up.

To say that I was somewhat less than enthusiastic about this plan would be an understatement.

"But I don't wanna go to a shrink in New York City."

"Carol, this is the man who saved my life. Dr. Paul Bernstein. He's a genius."

"But I don't wanna go to a shrink in New York City."

"Well, you want to stop sleepwalking, don't you?"

"Yes . . . but can't I do that without going to a shrink in New York City?"

But as you know, when you're eleven and your opponent is forty-nine and much taller, guess who wins?

You should remember, it wasn't like today, where children trade antidepressants on the playground like baseball cards. Back then, a kid going to a shrink was a very shameful scarlet-letter sort of deal. So I told no one. Not even my two best friends, who are still my best friends to this day.

So once a week after school, we headed to New York City for my shrinkage. Now, would my mother be bringing me into the city for my weekly appointment? Negative, sports fans. She left that task to my sixteen-year-old sister, Jane.

Off we schlepped each and every Thursday on the Long Island Rail Road to therapy land. Talk about not being like today! The thought now of an eleven-year-old girl and a sixteen-year-old girl traveling by themselves to New York City—well, it sounds only slightly less irresponsible than asking a guy on the subway to watch your purse.

Once we arrived at Penn Station, my sister was instructed to get us a cab to take us to the Second Coming's office on East Eighty-sixth Street, where I finally met the much buzzed-about Dr. Bernstein. And to say it was not kismet when we did meet would be putting it mildly. First, he was old—like, could-go-at-any-second old. With a big gut, a pasty face, and longish thinning gray hair. But the worst part came when he opened his tight-lipped mouth.

"Vat a pleasure to meet you, Keeral. Come in."

It was the worst German *Hogan's Heroes* accent you've ever heard.

"Von't you lie down here?"

Lie down?! Yes, Mother had also neglected to include that little fun fact in my orientation pack. I was young, but I knew somewhere that lying down in the presence of someone older who you didn't know very well was mucho creepy.

These sessions with Dr. Bernstein were quickly off to a bad start. First, he wanted me to free-associate.

"Just say vatever comes to mind."

"But what if nothing comes to mind?"

"Ve'll just vait until it does."

This became something of a challenge to a sixth grader who simply wanted to get home to watch *Batman* on channel seven. I would struggle and stammer through my allotted time. And then my sister would come pick me up after an hour of killing time at a nearby Schrafft's ice cream parlor.

When I got back home, there was never any discussion

with my mother, like "How's it going? Do you feel it's work-ing, making you better?" Nothing. Just the implicit assump-tion that I was to keep going. But still, that didn't hide my unhappiness. I heard tell that my parents found a note buried deep in my desk drawer on which I had scribbled in large capital letters: "I HATE DR. FATHEAD!"

The therapy continued all that spring. I dreaded Thurs-days every week, starting on the Friday mornings after, until one day when I made the decision that it would stop. Yes, like a cunning Jenga player, I knew somehow that one more strategically placed block could topple this tower. And if that was going to happen, I was going to be the sole archi-tect of it. And I was certain it was possible to ensure the de-struction of Dr. Fathead.

For one thing, I'd just seen a magician a week before on *The Merv Griffin Show* who'd gotten out of a straitjacket while locked in a trunk. And for another, I'd read most of the Nancy Drew series—and that teen could pretty much ac-complish anything with merely a bobby pin.

So one day, after much daydreaming in social studies during a scintillating discussion of state capitals, I decided my plan of attack. I would continue to go to Dr. Fathead. But with one very different element added to the equation— I would not speak.

I found out quickly that not speaking to a shrink was akin to going to a gynecologist and leaving your pantyhose on. Dr. Fathead wasn't happy.

"Don't you vant to talk about anything today?"

My stony silence had just the right alibi.

"My unconscious is just feeling quiet today, Herr Bernstein. Can't force it, can I?"

What could he say to that? Besides, lying on the couch meant that I wasn't facing him, so this was a much easier protest than I had imagined. I blissfully spent the rest of the session in my head dissecting the previous week's episode of *Batman,* which I had particularly enjoyed. How funny it was that Batman and Robin's enemy, Mr. Freeze, had offered them both some baked Alaska at the end when he was dressed like a regular person. That was good.

When my sister came to pick me up, Dr. Fathead was furious. "Your sister! She von't speak. She von't say anything!"

And Jane, justifiably unhappy in her own right about having to come here once a week as my travel pimp, just stared the doc down and said, "Well, what do you want *me* to do about it? Look, we got a train to catch." And making like a banana, we split.

Pretty soon, I did not have to go to Dr. Bernstein anymore. Mission accomplished—it was over and done. The sleepwalking had stopped long before, anyway.

Now, I love my mother a lot. I do. But I look back on this story and I think, *What on God's green earth was the woman thinking?* I'm sure the sleepwalking was just a product of having a lot of stress at the time, worried about making good grades while having a lot of extracurricular activities. And if my mother had sat me down and said, "What's going on? I'm concerned and I care. Let's have a good long talk about it," I believe it all could have been okay. Which is so ironic, *because that's exactly what she does for a living*. But why is it the shrinks have a much easier time of it with paying strangers?

To this day, this story is still difficult for me to recount. But as horrible as this experience was, it has also given me some of my greatest strengths. Many flowers have grown out of this weed called Dr. Bernstein. For example, I like to think that I am a nice person. When I leave the supermarket, I always walk my shopping cart back to the appropriate designated area. I never fail to replace an empty roll of toilet paper with a new one—even in public bathrooms. I pick up other people's trash on the street. Yes, I am *very* nice.

But . . . don't cross me. Do not. Because if you do, your face quickly morphs into that of Dr. Fathead. And it summons up in me a will of iron that cannot be broken. And to boot, I ain't eleven anymore.

This experience also demonstrated to me the power of silence. It's pretty potent stuff, keeping your yap shut. And I make an extra effort to remind myself of that, especially during those few seconds before I want to blow about something.

But more than anything, this episode gave me the confidence to know that in any problematic situation I encounter in my life, there is *always* a way out.

I know they say that when you get lemons, make lemonade. And I think that's what this story is ultimately about. But let's not forget that the overwhelming ingredient of lemonade is still lemons.

My mother was never really fond of a joke that I used to

do about her in my act years ago. It was, "It's hard to picture my mom solving other peoples' problems when she's the root of most of mine." But I'm sure that every kid who has a parent who's a shrink has felt the same thing. Why can't the professionals incorporate their expertise into their own lives?

There's that old saying, "The cobbler's children have no shoes." Is it just the nature of the beast? Maybe a dad who's an accountant is bad with math homework? Or the kid with the worst exhibit at the science fair has a father who's a scientist? Is it just the risk that every parent runs who has a career?

But keep that couch warm! The wheel keeps turning. If my kid turns out to think that I'm not all that funny, I might just very well be back one more time.

Preventative Medicine

The best day of my life was the twenty-four hours I thought I had cancer.

I was running late that day, but that had been pretty standard recently. Being in the throes of a passionate new love affair will do that to a girl. When you're seeing a member of the opposite sex, it's one thing—but when it's the first time you've "hopped the fence" and dated another female, that's an entirely different category of being out of it. But isn't that the whole point of a new infatuation? To legitimately have one's head in the clouds with no apologies?

So big deal if I arrived at three-fifteen instead of three. No worries, because I have an otherwise excellent track record when it comes to doctor appointments—I've never missed one in all my adult life. And that's not only because

I'm Jewish. I'm just one of those people who *like* going to the doctor.

So much so that back when I was a full-time stand-up comic, the maître d' in a club in New York City came over to me before a show one night and said, "Your doctor is in the audience tonight."

And I replied, "Doctor? Which one?" (Between the internist, gynecologist, dermatologist, ear-nose-and-throat guy, et al., the room could have been filled with nothing *but* doctors.)

See, I like going to the doctor because it means that I'm in charge. Sickness and disease don't stand a chance if you're all up in their Kool-Aid with diagnostic tests and preventative measures. (And I wasn't about to change that policy, my lesbo fling notwithstanding.)

Besides the fact that I especially like my radiologist, Dr. Behotek. The magazines in his waiting room are all up-to-date and top-of-the-line—like *People, Us Weekly,* and *Vanity Fair*—and not like the office copy of *Bone Density Today,* which some quacks think is all that. Also, Dr. Behotek's practice is in a really sweet corner of Beverly Hills. And afterward I like to reward myself for a clean bill of health by browsing the really cute shops that surround the doc's place.

Sure, it's a given that having the actual mammogram sucks. First, you have to wait around like an idiot in that paper robe-shirt. (The only time it's handy to wear this shmata is if you have your mammogram at lunchtime and bring in your own pastrami sandwich with extra Russian dressing.) Next, the female X-ray technician applies those Band-Aids to your nipples, which is such a nice hello! (And all you can think about when they go on is how much it's going to smart later when they get yanked off.)

But very soon the kindly tech, while wearing an illustrated "I Love Kitties" set of scrubs, quickly morphs into an X-ray-machine-wielding S&M dominatrix. Her one true mission in life turns out to be taking your formerly full and bouncy boobs and squashing them good with these heavy glass plates, trying her darnedest to make them into crepes. But you just hold your breath as instructed with each X-ray she takes, knowing that once she's through with her torture device, you won't have to be back for another year.

After the X-rays, I went back to the examining room and waited for the doc to come in and give me the rest of the normal drill—wherein he tells me that everything looks fine and then proceeds to feel me up real good for free. (It's quite a hoot because you both have to pretend like it's not happening.) The small talk while he soundly rounds second base is never short of classic:

"So, do you think that reality TV is slowly taking over sitcoms?"

"I'm not sure, Doc—but FYI, with that kneading technique you got going on there, you could make a mean loaf of bread!"

But that's not what happened this time.

The tech came in and said, "The doctor wants me to take a few more films of your left breast."

I felt a minute pang of anxiety, but I immediately shooed

it away. No biggie. (Who doesn't take two pictures just to be safe when you use your own camera?) So we took some more X-rays, and more time passed. Then the panic feeling poked its head out of its rabbit hole again, but I told him it was still way too early for him to make an appearance.

After what seemed like an eternity, the doctor came in and said seven words you never want to hear in a radiologist's office: "I see something on your X-ray here." My head was spinning and I tried to focus as he said he wanted to take a "needle aspiration" of the area to see what was inside, and that it could just be liquid, which I was told would be a good thing.

"And what if it's *not* liquid?" I asked.

"Well, then, we'll go from there."

He excused himself to go prepare, and I excused myself to go to the rest room. And once I was safely inside, I fell to my knees, closed my eyes, and clasped my two hands together—hard.

"Oh, God. Please, God. I'm begging you for this to be nothing. Please, God. Please. I'll do anything to be okay." (For someone who would have easily described herself as "holiday Jewish" at the time, I sure found religion real fast on the tile of that bathroom floor.)

I returned to the examining room to wait for the doctor to do the procedure. And that's when I called her: Lori, the woman I had just started seeing.

"Hello?"

"Hi. It's Carol." (We weren't quite yet up to saying "It's

me" yet.) "I'm at the doctor's office having my mammogram, and something's going on. They're giving me another
test and I'm really scared right now."

"Look, don't stress. Just stay calm and take it one step
at a time."

She was as cool as a cucumber.

"I know I should, but I'm kinda freaking!"

"Just breathe and try to stay in the moment. It'll all be
okay."

The amazing thing about an incident like this is that it
doesn't leave much time for thinking. You're operating on a
purely visceral level. So why did I call her first instead of my
family back in New York? I'll never really know. I guess my
adrenaline made that choice.

The doctor walked in, and I hurriedly had to hang up.
But those twenty seconds Lori and I had had on the phone
had definitely soothed me.

The doctor did the needle aspiration, examined it, and
said, "It's not a liquid."

Not what I wanted to hear.

"We'll have to send it off to the lab to be tested. I'll get
the results back tomorrow morning, around ten. And then
we can go from there." (That infernal "going from there"
again—these doctors love to get all MapQuest on you when
they get bad news.)

I went back to the changing room and put on my clothes,
still trying to keep a tight lid on my burgeoning panic and
fear.

Then, as I passed the doctor on the way out, something made me stop him in his tracks. "So, what's your feeling, Dr. Behotek? What do you think it is?"

Dr. Behotek took a beat and said, "I think it's probably cancerous."

"Like, fifty-fifty?"

"No, like, eighty-twenty."

"How do you know that?"

"From thirty years of doing what I do."

My body jumped to the front of the panic parade, and I started feeling numb. It's weird. You're breathing and walking and obviously moving, but you only know that because you haven't collapsed.

And that's the moment it started—the immediate demarcation between Before and Now. Before: as in earlier that morning when I had been running late and had been such a space cadet that I'd only noticed at the doctor's office that I had put on just one hoop earring. Before: as in yesterday when I was thinking about what to buy Lori for a Chanukah present. Before: as in when I was carefree and happy, not a worry in the world. And Now: when I am not.

Now was cancer and only cancer. And I started to think about all the silly things I got upset about, during Before: like when someone hadn't returned a phone call. (Did that really upset me that much the other day?) And the tailor ruining a pair of pants that I loved. (Why did I go ballistic over that? What for?) The woman in the car in front of me on my way over to the mammogram, doing three miles an hour. (Did I really need to blast her so hard with my horn?)

I went home to my apartment and called my parents, sister, and brother back on the East Coast. Then I had a big long cry by myself, reducing to a giant ball an entire box of Kleenex tissues, all the while thinking, *How did this happen? This was supposed to be just an ordinary day. Why aren't I at those shops now trying on something I can't afford in order to celebrate my clean mammogram?*

Then an odd thing happened. I started to blame my boobs as well. I felt as if they were somehow implicated in this diagnosis.

"So let me get this straight, girls. You two are my most treasured physical asset and you let *cancer* get in?! I gave you thorough exams regularly in the shower—you know that! This, after all those exquisite lacy French black bras I bought you? After all those push-ups—the exercise, not the bras—I do to keep you firm and high? Ingrates!"

Lori came right over after work. She walked in carrying a giant basket full of movie DVDs and snacks. Then she hugged me for a supremely long time.

And it was then that I knew I was covered.

I was safe.

I would be okay.

She said she'd brought the basket because she thought it just might be fun to chill, hang out, and watch movies all night. It would maybe take my mind off of everything. But I said that what I really wanted to do was go out and get drunk. Blotto drunk. And she was fine with that.

So we went to this place that we had found in the midst of our three-week courtship where they served kick-ass apple martinis—and I began my long journey that night by draining several of them.

"What if I have breast cancer?"

"We'll deal with it."

"We'll." Did you hear that? She just said "We'll."

"What if I have to lose part of my breast or have a mastectomy?"

"What I really think you should be more focused on right now is eating some more bread. Have something in your stomach to soak up all those cocktails."

And as I proceeded to progressively anesthetize myself, she was the rock. I needed to fall apart and she let me, this woman who I wouldn't even have called my "girlfriend" yet for fear of moving too fast and blowing it.

The evening ended and I was sufficiently plastered, as requested. Lori put me in the passenger seat of her car and safely deposited me back home. Then she put me to bed and I passed out in a sweet oblivion.

I woke up the next morning, and Lori had already left for work. But she'd left me a note saying she'd thought it was better to let me sleep and that I should call her the minute I got the results from the doctor. So I got up and, even with one hell of a hangover, I prepared. I prepared to have cancer.

I made the bed and mentally readied myself to be strong and tough and a warrior. I ate my cornflakes and decided I wasn't going to let anything beat me down. Cancer was definitely doable. But the best piece of news that I hadn't known just one day earlier was: I could do anything or beat anything if Lori was by my side.

Ten A.M. came, and I literally sat by the phone. Stared right at it as if we were locked in the world's biggest staring contest. Then a few minutes later, the phone rang and it was the doctor.

"I have great news. The tumor turned out to be what's called a fibroadenoma. It's the most common benign tumor."

And I exhaled the biggest apple-martini-tinged exhale of my life.

The rest of his monologue was a bit foggy, as my mind was overflowing with joy. I did catch him saying, though, that I still had to have the tumor removed, and that was a definite. But he assured me that within a year or so of the procedure, there would probably not even be any kind of mark left.

I called Lori and my family to share the good news and I cried the "happy" cry (knowing that Now had gone back to being Before).

I have told this story many times over the years, and uniformly the first thing people always say is, "What kind of schmuck radiologist relays an eighty percent malignant cancer scenario before he even gets the results back? Didn't you just want to scream? Didn't you just want to run right to his office and rip his head off?"

And the answer is always a resounding "No."

Look, I'm the one who flagged him down on the way out. I'm the one who solicited his hunch. I take full blame for being an inquisitive noodge. But more important than all that—he found it. (Yes, the tumor turned out to be benign, but they're still potential trouble if they stay.)

No, far from being angry, I am so grateful for that day. I think back to it constantly, and I have never lived my life the same since. Now did go back to Before, although down on my knees on that bathroom floor, I did strike a lot of bargains. And a deal's a deal in my book, even if it was made under false pretenses.

And the deal points were these: number one—realizing that my life is truly glorious, and I am a lucky, lucky girl. I need to appreciate that stone-cold fact so much more than I already do. Number two—I must stop getting bogged down in the minutiae of life (like when altered pants don't turn out right or people drive like turtles). And lastly, number three, my good health is still something to strive for every day, but never *ever* to be taken for granted.

So why did it take a cancer scare for me to learn all this? It doesn't really matter now. But I can tell you that my compass sure changed direction after that day.

But the biggest surprise was what this experience did for my relationship with Lori. And I know that fateful day was a blessing. Because I saw the beacon of Lori's true character and, as a result, fell in love with her so much earlier than I was supposed to.

I think back and oftentimes wonder, if the tables had been turned, would I have stepped up to the plate as effortlessly as she did? I'm afraid I might have been pretty spooked. Lucky girl, indeed.

So I did have the fibroadenoma taken out, and I went back to New York to do it. (We New York Jews are very loyal to our New York MDs.) And Lori came back with me (no surprise, I'm sure, at this point).

We went to Long Island to see my folks the day before the procedure—even though I hadn't told my parents about our relationship yet. I just told them that Lori was my "friend" who had come along for moral support. And I didn't feel guilty about saying that. This was purely the non-cancerous-tumor trip—plenty of time to do the coming-out chore when I was ready on some other visit.

And when I did finally go back to Long Island a few months later to come out to my folks, my mother was not surprised in the least. She told me she knew right away when Lori came with me to Long Island. I asked my mother how and she said that when we all took a walk together in the neighborhood that afternoon, that's when she could tell.

"The way you two were walking together, I could feel your connection."

And she was right.

So, yes, I still like going to the doctor. It's as true as ever to me, that "ounce of prevention" stuff. (But the follow-up questions to the doc as I'm leaving? Those I definitely skip now.)

It's funny how just another day can quickly turn into the most important day of your life. But now I simply try to make sure that just another day and the most important day are always the same day.

Minimum Wage

I have always loved working. And I had both my parents as great role models to thank for that. My mother started working when I was in grade school, and my dad not only worked a full-time job in the city, but at night saw patients at his home office. In fact, it was my father who gave me my first glimpse into the working world.

On school holidays, as early as first grade, my father would cart me and my older sister off with him to New York City to his optical office near Penn Station. Once there, our chore was pretty simple—to clean the display cases that housed the eyeglasses frames. So, armed with a small spray bottle, a roll of paper towels, and some good old kiddie elbow grease, a young worker bee was born.

For the perks alone, it was well worth the trip: the exciting rush-hour ride into the city on the Long Island Rail Road (change at Jamaica!), the stop at the nearby E. J. Korvette's store in Herald Square to pick out the record album of our choice, and lunch at the world-famous Automat (where it was quite thrilling to be handed a big stack of coins to put in slots so you could pick out the food you wanted from behind dozens of glass panels—very empowering for a seven-year-old who was used to eating whatever was shoved in front of her).

As soon as six o'clock came, we packed up our stuff to head home. But before we left, my father paid us three dollars each. But not just any three dollars—three dollars in sealed yellow pay envelopes made out to each of us, our full names in bold black letters. And, these many years later, that envelope still has an effect on me. My father certainly could have just handed us the money (or not paid us at all, for that matter), but he elevated our menial task to something special by putting the money in that yellow pay envelope.

So soon afterward, when I became a Brownie, it was no surprise when I got all hopped up at the prospect of selling Girl Scout Cookies. (And this was when you didn't have to send your kid out microchipped and accompanied by a bodyguard.) So I set out into our neighborhood, primed to be the top seller of my troop, and everything was going swimmingly—until I got to one particular house. The woman who answered the door ordered three boxes, and, at a quarter apiece (let's not forget, I did mention an Automat!), I relayed that the total was seventy-five cents. She handed me a dollar bill, but I just stood there, confused.

"I said it's seventy-five cents, ma'am."

"Yes, dear, I know. I just gave you a dollar, and in return you give me twenty-five cents."

Seemed that before I'd ventured out into the world as a mini "Wilma" Loman, no one had bothered to explain the concept of "change." So I was pretty steamed at this lady. Did she think I had just rolled off the tomato truck yesterday? I wasn't about to fall for that "I give you this, then you give me that" scam. So I waved her off and left her house, disappointed by yet another snarky grown-up. (And to think those three boxes would have gotten me awfully close to beating smooth-talking Renee Greco as first-place salesperson.)

The next time there was an opportunity for employment wasn't until high school. I was very bored back then, and I figured it this way—I could hang out, or I could hang out and get paid (which was a job). So I did some investigating. Two of my girlfriends told me that their boss was looking for more employees at the local Roy Rogers. So I applied and was quickly hired.

My tenure at Roy Rogers started out rather well. I was given a uniform to wear (so I didn't have to sully my own personal very cool, very hip peasant shirts and Landlubber jeans). Also, I was allowed to eat whatever chow of theirs I wanted on meal breaks (and as a ravenous teenager with a sizable tapeworm, I took full advantage of that).

Granted, there were some things that bugged me. When customers came up to the counter, I had to robotically recite the company-dictated "Howdy, partner! How may I serve you?" (All while wearing a cowgirl outfit topped off by a red felt cowboy hat.) And when the patrons left, I was made to shout gleefully after them, "Happy Trails!" But who cared? I was making a dollar ninety an hour, which was all going toward my intended dream car—a Pontiac Firebird—and I could take whatever was dished out just by thinking about that prize at the bottom of the Cracker Jack box.

But soon things started to get a little tricky, because I came to learn that the customers *spoke*. And not only spoke, but were customers from Greenvale, a very upscale neighborhood on Long Island and a town no stranger to the word "yenta." And, like most yentas, these women were not lacking in needs.

For example, there was the very well-dressed woman with tons of jewelry who came in every day holding her bichon frise and always ordered the same thing: "A roast beef. No bun. No sauce. If there's a speck of sauce on it, I'll make you take it right back. It's the only thing my Muffin will eat." (About a month into the job, I realized that Muffin was the dog.)

Besides that piece of work, there were other assorted high-maintenance looney bins who said things like, "I want fries, but just the crispier, more well-done ones. Don't give me any that are still beige or, God forbid, white."

These constant individual requests started to become very wearing to me. *This is a fast-food joint, people,* I would think, *not a high-class place like Steak 'N Brew!*

To make matters worse, a sardonic mind-set toward the customer was already in my genes. You see, my optometrist father had always regaled the family with stories of clueless patients. Like when he told a man to read the eye chart and the guy asked, "Out loud?"

Or he told us about people who would read the eye chart and say, "Capital *E,* capital *F,* capital *C.*"

"They're *all* capitals, numbnuts!"

So wasn't it just a matter of time before I snapped?

Here's what happened. A woman came in and ordered a hamburger and french fries. I told her the burger was ready and the french fries would be coming along a minute later. In the meantime, I rang another customer, and then *one minute later*—as promised—when the fries "came up," as we say in the fast-food trade, I placed them down on the woman's tray next to her burger.

"I want a new burger now."

"A new burger. Why?"

First mistake. Questions to the customer can only lead to trouble.

"Because the burger's not hot enough now."

We stared each other down for a few seconds, and then out it came.

"Oh, come on, lady. This burger's still plenty hot."

I was quickly shuffled to the back office of Roy Rogers (really just a small room where they kept the extra buns) and was asked to turn in my uniform. (Like I was gonna keep it.) Then I was surprised to hear that this bust had actually not been my first infraction at Roy Rogers. Evidently, a couple of weeks earlier, a corporate spy had been sitting in his car in the parking lot observing me through the window during a slow stretch and had caught me eating directly from the french fry tray. "Big Cowboy" had been watching!

So I vowed that at my next job I would zip it and zip it good. No need to get my panties all in a wad. I saw clearly that success in a job came down to accepting your role as a ventriloquist's dummy with someone else's hand up your ass.

I took my next job literally a hundred yards away from the Roy Rogers as a cashier at a Pathmark supermarket. (My salary was then up to two dollars and five cents an hour.) I was intrigued by this job because it demanded "training." (Maybe that was what had gone wrong at the O.K. Corral. I had not been properly schooled.)

So for an entire weekend, I attended their Pathmark "training academy." It felt elite and special, like being part of the grocery Mossad, and I learned all sorts of stuff: like which items were taxable and which were not (which I still remember to this day—and FYI, if something is labeled "medicated," it's not taxable), and the proper way to bag groceries. And there was some skill involved with all of this that kept it interesting—especially since this was all before scanners.

At the beginning, it was tough. Every other item you picked up, you had to look to the old pro checker like an ignorant dweeb and ask, "Mary? How much?"

And with barely a glance up, Mary would blurt out the price immediately, "Dellwood half-gallon-size milk? Forty-four cents, doll."

But lo and behold, with time I got faster and faster, and soon *I* was the expert people asked for price checks. I really dug that job. But then my mother got me a tutoring job over the summer for five dollars an hour (which was Trump change at the time), so I bolted from the grocery world. And when the summer was over, it felt sort of passé to go back.

Then one of my best friends, Cathy, who was working as a waitress at the local IHOP, said they needed a hostess. My ears pricked up at this.

Hostess! I thought. *What a lovely elevation of my station. I wouldn't be running around like a waitress with her head cut off. No need to confront or provoke. Just seat and ring up!*

I had just one special set of instructions given to me by my manager, a man who called himself simply Mr. D.

"If a bill is more than twenty-five dollars, give the party their normal change, but make sure to ring only twenty-five dollars on the register. Got it?"

"Got it, Mr. D.!"

Believe me, he could have said, "When you see on a bill that someone has ordered pigs in a blanket, hop up and down on one foot while ringing it up," and I would have said, "Absolutely."

So one Sunday morning—the 'Nam of the pancake world—I was spinning plates. And as I rang up a bill for a rather large church group, a nice gentleman in a suit stood casually by the register and made some pleasant small talk. I was slightly peeved because I was so swamped, but nothing was going to sway me now from my new docile Toni Tennille personality. A few minutes later, the nice man made a comment.

"I just noticed that party of twenty that just left here? I'm sure their bill was pretty big, but you only rang up twenty-five dollars on the cash register."

And I instantly replied, "Well, of course I did, sir! Because that's what my manager, Mr. D., instructed me to do." And as another large group entered, fresh from a morning softball game, I excused myself politely and grabbed a bunch of menus to greet them.

Well, apparently, corporate spies were de rigueur for every large corporation at the time, and wasn't I quite the magnet for all of them? But I completely assumed that since I had done nothing technically wrong and I was just doing what I'd been told, I would escape any repercussions. But I was very much wrong. I heard they ripped Mr. D. a new one pretty good, but for some reason, he wound up staying at IHOP.

And the hostess with the mostest? Well, I didn't get fired. I just wound up not getting any more hours. (Socrates and Plato could have easily done an hour on that one.) And for a couple of weeks, like an idiot, I would go into IHOP to look at the schedule, find my name, and follow the line across the sheet with my finger—and find it blank. I wanted to kick myself. How could I possibly have wound up trusting a man who went by a last name that was just a letter?

So needless to say, I never did get that Firebird. But I did learn that it's basically a lose-lose in the minimum-wage world: If you use your instinctual skeptic's nature, you get canned. If you become a head-nodding automaton, you get canned, too.

(Thank the Lord that I found the world of comedy. Sarcastic attitude? Check! Be provocative and right in people's faces? Double check!)

But I'm still grateful for those early days in the minimum-wage trenches. They taught me a lot of lessons that I still rely on today, like: Don't take things personally with customers' idiotic requests. Less information shared is always better than more. Scheming bosses have a tendency to fail upward. And everybody needs their version of the yellow envelope at the end of each working day—simply an affirmation that they are valuable and doing a good job.

And maybe I still always pay for a box of Girl Scout Cookies with exact change, too.

The *I* in "Team"

I have been with my partner, Lori, for twelve years. And when it's completely legal for two chicks to get married, we will. (We love parties, especially ones about us. Plus the idea of forcing strangers to eat side by side for a few awkward hours is also very appealing.)

Being in this relationship makes me especially happy, because it's one less thing I have to worry about in life. Like, when I watch these reality shows with people desperately trying to find the person they want to spend the rest of their lives with, I just sit back, smile, and say, "Good luck, folks. I'm done!"

But I severely underestimated one element of this couple situation. I had no idea beforehand how big a role compromise would play. Because that's what any long-term relationship ultimately becomes—a constant negotiation.

The stuff of life needs to be divvied up. Especially with two women together, where there are questions that otherwise, in a typical male-female pairing, probably wouldn't even need to be broached. Like:

Who drives when we're both in the car? She does.

If there's a dead bird outside, who will dispose of it? She will.

Who knows how to shut off the water in the house? She does.

But before you start sensing a theme here . . .

Who will scoop up a spider in the bathroom and put it outside? I will.

Who would fire someone who works in the house? I would.

(Who cooks dinner? Neither one of us.)

And I'm also the one who keeps the social calendar, sends out all the change-of-address and holiday cards, and the one who calls the city to report a pothole. In fact, I'm happy to make any and all calls from this day forward, so long as I never have to go outside and find any switches, knobs, panels, or valves—much less fiddle with them in the dark.

But then there are those compromises in couplehood that are not so simple, because the individual personality quirks kick in. Then it gets a little tricky. For example, what do you do when two people have completely different needs temperature-wise in the bedroom? Lori prefers a warm and toasty bedroom, a bedroom that has the feeling of, say, a chick-hatching facility. Whereas I like it *normal*.

So our bedroom at night quickly transforms into a vaudeville stage act. I get up to open a window.

"Don't do that, Carol. The alarm is on."

"I know, but it's so hot in here."

"Well, then, turn off the alarm, but open the window just a crack—because I'm freezing."

I open the window, but then she proceeds to get up and throw yet another comforter onto her side of the bed.

"That thing is so bulky, Lori. You're gonna smother the dogs."

"Well, you can take off the comforter, Carol, but then will you put the heat up for me just the tiniest smidge?"

"Of course, sweetheart."

And then I remove the comforter, go over to the thermostat outside our bedroom door, and pretend to put the heat on. Because a sturdy tenet I've come to learn about being in it for the long haul is, "What she doesn't know won't kill her."

Oh, the white lies! I dare any half of a couple who's been together ten-plus years to say they haven't dallied in this:

"Did you stop at the dry cleaner's today, honey?"

"Oh, I tried but they were closed already."

(When, in fact, the cleaners were very much open, but I just really wanted a frozen yogurt instead—which, of course, I spilled on my blouse, meaning I had to go back to the dry cleaner's the next day anyhow.)

"Did you call that guy about fixing the speakers in the living room?"

"Yeah, I left a message for him."

(When, truth be told, I never even dialed the guy, because I was on the brink of finally cracking the Puzzlemaster's Sunday challenge on NPR, which is pretty remarkable, considering it was so hard to hear because there's something wrong with our speakers.)

White lies are like the packing peanuts of any relationship. Because, in the end, what's a white lie here and there when you're a rock-solid team? *That's* the essential ingredient for the long haul. 'Cause there ain't no *I* in "team," people!

You know the drill. You become your own private Mafia. Like, say, when your partner has someone who's "dead" to them, then they gotta be dead to you, too. No way around it, Vito. Even if your partner was wrong in whatever happened with this person, it doesn't matter, because that's what's in the rule book.

And I am so grateful that we're on the same page politically, too—which is no small feat. Take a couple like James Carville and Mary Matalin. (The liberal Democrat with the right-wing conservative?) I swear, I don't get how they do it without ripping each other's hair out. (On second thought, looking at Carville, maybe they're not doing so well after all.)

Look, I know I could compromise on a lot of things. For example, Lori and I are both Jewish. But if someone's faith mattered that much to them at their core, I would have no problem being with someone not Jewish.

But to me, it's your politics that represent your real core beliefs and your entire value system. And how could you not share those with the person you're spending your life with?

Which brings to light the new issue that has thrown a curveball into my entire concept of compromise. I recently became vegan. (Note to Hallmark: Is this a new greeting card opportunity?) For years, I had been inching closer to making the move but just never took the plunge. But then the writers' strike happened and I suddenly had all this time to read the books I'd always wanted to, and watch all the animal videos I'd never wanted to (but finally summoned up the courage for). And then, once I made the connection between animals and the food I was eating and all the clothes and products I was using, there was no turning back.

So, of course, now I'm looking for my team! There's nothing I want more than for Lori to saddle up (in a non-leather saddle, of course) and ride right alongside me on this passionate endeavor. But, as it turns out, my passion is not quite hers yet. Oh, sure, she's been very supportive in going to all these new vegan restaurants with me—which, by the way, are also great places to check out the new Priuses—and in picking up cool foods for me to try that she knows I can eat—but her jury's still out. And I'm left in a very discombobulated state because *we need to feel the same things.*

Quite unexpectedly, this experience is giving me a whole new appreciation for Tom Cruise. I remember reading that when he first hooked up with Katie Holmes, Tom immediately sent her off to the Scientology training center. I recall thinking that was a bit freaky. But I totally get it now. Because when you become so impassioned about a certain way of life, body and soul, your next thought instantly becomes that your partner's gotta feel the love, too. Hey, other people can eat meat till the cows come (or don't come) home. But I sure do care now whether my one and only does.

And it's led to some uncomfortable dinners as of late. Like:

"Lori, how can you possibly eat that steak after I showed you that video from the slaughterhouse?"

"Can we not talk about this now, Carol?"

"See, that's the problem! 'Steak.' We don't call it what it really is, to remove people as far away as possible from the animal experience."

"Are you almost done, sweets, because I am really losing my appetite here?"

"Well, that was kinda the point, hon."

And what's so ironic in all this is that Lori was the first link in the chain that led me down this path. She created the animal lover where once there was none! I never had a pet as a kid, and was just basically unmoved by animals. But Lori had a dog and two cats when we got together. And as much as it pains me now to say this, I couldn't have cared less about them. So much so that when we finally made the decision to move in together, I made it firm that other friends and family would have to take care of them. It was my deal breaker.

But when I saw that Lori was actually prepared to make this sacrifice for our relationship to move forward, I just couldn't do it. So move in they did, and, with time, I came to love them as my own. And through loving them, all animals became one to me along the same continuum. So how did the one who was so far behind on the track, dawdling aimlessly while the other ran a twelve-minute mile, wind up becoming the marathon runner?

And yet, this is what I love best about relationships. You never know what's 'round the bend—and it sure does keep it interesting. Yeah, the thermostat disputes, the errands tally, whatever, turn out to be the easy stuff. But how do I live with someone who still eats meat? How does *she* live with someone who stopped? What diet will we give to our son? Guess we'll find out.

Yeah, it's still all about teamwork—that's the constant. But as it turns out, there is a lot of *I* in "team." And that's a good thing, because it means that you're both still thinking and growing. The trunk stays rooted but the branches veer off here and there. And I believe that makes it a lovelier tree.

So I'll keep trying. I will. (Like, if I show her this one video of how they make foie gras, I know I have a real shot.)

But, come to think of it, I'm the one who could learn a lesson or two from Lori's old playbook. Like, did she freak out ten years ago when I said I couldn't live with her animals? Did she say, "I absolutely cannot compromise on that—that's *my* deal breaker," even though I'm sure that's how she felt? No. She just went with love and let me find my own answers. Pretty crafty of her, eh?

And I need to remember that this new lifestyle choice

was also predicated on becoming a more humane and compassionate person. And, as it has turned out, not just toward the animals—but toward the humans, too.

I just hope the fake chicken ("Ficken"!) that Lori prepared for me last night was really that. She'd be crazy not to have some white lies of her own, right?

So Long, Friend

Dear Friend,

So let me get this straight. No note. No call. No heads-up whatsoever. You just up and leave me? Geez, I thought I would've gotten the teensiest bit more notice before you bolted like that.

Am I disappointed? Completely. Did I expect more because we go way back how many years? Absolutely.

I can't help but think back to the beginning now. I remember how anxious I was to first meet you. And how all my little girlfriends were atwitter as well. You were so popular that you were even the star of your very own movie that detailed every little fun fact there was to know about you.

I vividly recall that day in fifth grade when they carted

off only us girls to see that flick—so exclusive that the boys weren't even allowed admission.

"Your body is going through lots of changes now, girls. Changes you can't ignore. Hair will appear under your arms and on your lower abdomen."

Lower abdomen?! Is this film about our new friend or about us turning into werewomen?

Most of the girls in my class already had you as their friend. But not me. I just had to sit tight and dream of all the things we were going to do together once you anointed me a young lady.

And then, eureka! You finally made your appearance while I was away at summer camp. And pretty soon after, I was thinking what most girls did when they got to know you up close and personal: *Gee, quite the big buildup, but she really turns out to be just a royal pain!*

Because, back in those days, you stopped me from doing a lot of my favorite activities: swimming, horseback riding, water-skiing. And you required so much sophisticated equipment. Pads and belts—yikes! But worse, you brought along an otherworldy, new kind of pain to experience: cramps. Doubling me over in agony, how the hell did you whip those up? I soon came to learn that, much like a soloist at the Met, you were one high-maintenance diva.

And not only did you wreak havoc when you were around, but the week before your arrival—well, that was the real doozie. Boy, you sure knew how to turn me into a fire-breathing she-devil, didn't you? And the mood swings?

Transforming me from sparkly people person to heaping sobbing mess in two seconds flat.

No, I'll never understand what it was in that hormonal bag of tricks of yours that could assure me it was just fine and dandy to eat an entire box of Entenmann's chocolate donuts two days before your next visit. Then sometimes making me so bloated and puffy that, lying down on my back on my bed, I couldn't even get the fly zippered on my "fat pants."

But, to be fair, it is difficult not to look back and reminisce on some of the good times, too. Remember how many times you got me out of gym class in high school? I think that was the first time I officially called you my friend in public.

"Coach Wilson, I can't play volleyball today. I have my . . . friend."

Not another word needed to be said. The mere mention of our unwavering bond and—*poof*—goodbye, dorky gym uniform. (I got even better results telling this to a male teacher. So flummoxed were they at the mere mention of you, I'm surprised I didn't push to be excused for the entire semester.)

Yeah, we definitely had the classic love-hate thing going, didn't we? First I'd detest you and curse the day you ever came my way. Then I'd bow down and kiss your feet every time you showed up, relieved that I wasn't about to take on the role of Mommy without any rehearsal whatsoever.

Regardless of whatever excuse I could conjure up that

month (wrong-size diaphragm, an unfortunate encounter with "Mr. I'll Pull Out! I Promise I Will!," or my old standby "Just got drunk and dumb"), you still had this chick on her knees endlessly imploring you to come rescue me "this one last time, I swear!" I'm sure you just chuckled at all my penances.

And that time I went on the Pill, I confess now that I never felt quite right about it—even though I was told I was giving you a nice break. Every month, there you were like clockwork (very unlike you), but so weak and at a fraction of your former self. It made me sad to see you that way. I felt as if I'd somehow betrayed you.

But here we are today. And I'll admit it, I miss you, girl. I do! Look, I'm no dummy. I was aware that we were slowing down. (Please, I was dropping eggs faster than a waitress with Parkinson's during the breakfast rush at Denny's.) But my mother's friend left her when she was well into her fifties, so I was relying on a similar experience there. So when you bid me farewell at forty-seven? You really caught me off guard there, lady.

After you split, I asked myself a lot of questions. Since you made me a woman to begin with, I'm sure you were able to deduce what the first question was: With the baby-making wiring gone, what kind of female am I now?

But I can say unequivocally that I'm still the real deal. Because here's the kick in the pants: I have a baby now. So you may have closed up shop, but it didn't matter—because that's the beauty of adoption. (And the beauty of having the balls to go ahead with it at fifty.)

So, it's so long, friend. We had a good long ride together, huh? (Although the number you did on me with that tight white pantsuit that time? Well, that was just plain mean.) And to bring you up to speed, you'll be happy to know that my ovaries just bought a lovely condo down in Boca Raton, Florida. (They claim the shows they get at the clubhouse are better than on Broadway!)

Well, I don't want to make this goodbye any more awkward than it already is, so I've got to get going. I want to pick up a pair of these things they call "wicking pajamas." Have you heard of them? They're made with this fabric that promises to keep you cool all night. It's the darnedest thing: Since you left, someone keeps turning up the thermostat in my body without asking permission first. And these power surges are driving me loco. So you might be gone, but apparently some new royal pain moved in for me to contend with now.

And I'm sure you're busy, too. No doubt running off somewhere to ruin some sixteen-year-old's pool party. No worries. She'll get over it.

We all do.

The Body Grabs the Mike

At the halfway mark of my life as a woman, a strange feeling started to overtake me. I found that after countless years of shrink visits, Marianne Williamson seminars, and assorted courses at the Learning Annex, it all started to finally come together. I can now say with some confidence that I know who I am and know what I want unequivocally.

We're thrown a lot of gloom and doom about aging, us gals, but what they don't tell you is that the mind comes into a really good place. The stuff I've strived so hard in my life to accomplish is suddenly working. Finally, no, I don't need everyone to like me. And "Don't sweat the small stuff"? Piece of cake now, folks. I care so much less about so much more, it's staggering. Years on this planet will show you that. Good work, head! Mazel tov!

So, then, why is it that just when you're clicking on all cylinders, mistress of your own domain, finally truly comfortable in your own skin, the body turns on you? Turns on you like week-old potato salad.

The first thing the body decides to do midway through life is to show you, in no uncertain terms, who's the boss—and it ain't Tony Danza. Especially when it comes to trying something new. You go to the body and make a request. But the body can't hide its immediate condescending tone:

"You want to *what*? Take a Hot Grooves Funk Dance class at your local gym? Shake your moneymaker like you did back in the day? Sure, I guess I got no problem with that. But I *will* make sure you won't be able to walk the next day. Yeah, it'll look like you've got a pole stuck up your ass for about a week there. But who am I to say no when a precious flower such as yourself wants to bring 'sexy' back?"

The physical requires a visa of some sort after forty. My similarly aged buddy Lee met me for lunch recently looking much like a Picasso painting. His right shoulder was all hunched up while his left hip seemed to have completely left the country. I asked him what happened, and he literally said to me, "I reached for a box of cereal."

When you were twelve years old, you navigated your way around a game of Twister like Gumby. But now, a blast-from-the-past encounter like that could send you screaming to the emergency room. I swear, at this age, if you point a little too emphatically, you will feel it the next day.

Who knows why, but after forty the body develops a wicked sense of humor. Its dream of one day becoming a stand-up comic suddenly takes flight—and it starts acting out like a deranged little Chucky doll. Especially to us gals. It spends countless all-nighters dreaming up ways to seriously harass us.

Let's start with the subject of hair. Like I haven't spent enough time already in my life plucking, tweezing, waxing, and chasing down all my fuzzy slackers. But no, the body throws a boomerang in there late in the game. I like to call it, in deference to the great Neil Diamond, the "Solitary Man" hair. It's different from the rest, a troublemakin' type—thick, coarse, and wiry—with a devil-may-care attitude. Round and round it goes, and where it stops, nobody knows! It might take a stroll with no map whatsoever, get lost, and wind up down by a nipple perhaps. (What a turn-on for your panting partner.) Or hop aboard a train headed for the face and settle down deep in the valley of your chin. Once landed, it feels frisky and starts a challenging round of hide and seek.

"Thought you got me there, didn't ya? Well, think again! You might want to sharpen those tweezers if you're gonna go toe-to-toe with me, little lady!"

Which brings us to the mac daddy of all the aging ravages—your sight. My formerly 20/20 vision could have lasered in on this lone scallywag in two seconds flat, but now the eyes *don't* have it. My dream of follicular manslaughter suddenly goes up in smoke. Find a hair? Please, merely paying a dinner bill has become an aerobic pursuit at this point, with my hand moving close, then back, umpteen times.

"Is that a three or an eight on that total? Who the hell

knows? Can someone just point me in the direction of the line where I sign?" Oh, the down payments I've lost because my ego refused to take out those damn reading glasses.

The worst part is when the body gets the mind in on its evil schemes. I can't tell you how many times I've been in the shower, and just as I'm getting out, I'm wondering, *Did I just wash my face in there? I have a vague recollection, but it's all such a soapy mish-mosh now.*

And just when I think the body might be running out of gas, it stops and refuels, continuing its rampage. Like a newly minted frat boy armed with a twenty-four-pack of toilet paper on Halloween, it goes for broke. The body pulls out a megaphone:

"Listen up, hips and thighs! You handled all the candy and ice cream up till this point. Good work! But you're off duty now. I'd like to redirect everything to just the stomach now, please." Oh, tummy. Once firm and supple ground, now a mere Glad bag at the bottom of my body.

Why, body, why? What's with the relentlessness? Why do you suddenly take the soles of my once soft feet and make them all rough and cracked? I guess your eyes are going, too. Have you mistaken me for a Mr. Fred Flintstone? He needs his feet to drive a car, whereas I don't. Why do you take the parts of my arms that are supposed to be triceps and turn them into crepe paper? I'm not planning any par-ties. And why is everything just so damn *lumpy* now?

My body is having the last laugh and has become a bet-ter comedian than I could ever be. And the worst part is, like any good performer who's killing, I can't bear to drag her offstage. So I guess I'll just have to sit back and enjoy the show from the audience. What else can I do when the old bod just brought back adult acne last week? You gotta find the humor. (Or at least, find the humor at being the oldest person at my local pharmacy to ask for the whereabouts of the Clearasil.)

Oh, well. At least this funny chick had the decency to comp my front and center seat for her show.

But wait a minute—is that a nine or a six on my ticket? And am I in row one, or is it the letter *I*? Hmmm . . .

Soul to Sole

Everyone had told me what to expect when a parent dies: the usual suspects—shock, disbelief, sadness, denial. What they neglected to mention was that when they go after eighty-six years, they forget to take all their stuff.

So what to do with all of it? My dad's home office was a cinch to pack up. It was an optical office, crafted forty years ago from our family's former garage, so that after working a full-time day job in New York City, he returned home every evening to treat patients in the neighborhood. My mother, sister, brother, and I decided to donate Dad's leftover frames to charity—that was a no-brainer. Dad was one optometrist who had an overwhelming love and commitment to eye-wear—he was so committed, in fact, that he never even sold contact lenses in his private practice. "Why would any person wear contact lenses," he'd demand, "when there are so many attractive frames out there to choose from?"

Dad prided himself on being a one-stop shop when it came to prescribing glasses. My siblings and I grew up with *whiz* and *screech* sounds coming from the other end of the house, where his behemoth lens-cutting machines smoothed out the rough edges of delicate glass. So we donated his equipment to charity, too, confident that my father would be pleased to know that some newbie was learning his trade on his broken-in machines. I could almost hear him saying, "Kid, if you've got a business, know it from start to finish, inside and out, and upside down. *That's* when you know your field."

Optometry was my father's passion for sixty years (how could it not be, with a name like Seymour—you know, SEE MORE?), and it affected the way he looked at the world. He had an optical explanation for practically everything he encountered in life. This was never more apparent than when the O. J. Simpson case erupted. On the evening of her death, Nicole Simpson arrived safely at home after eating dinner at the restaurant where Ron Goldman worked, but she'd left her glasses behind. Goldman returned them to her nearby townhouse, and everyone knows how the rest of the grisly story unfolded. What was my father's solution for how the entire tragedy could have been avoided? "It's a testament to having two pairs of glasses. If she'd had a second pair at home, the two of them might both be alive today!"

Once we'd dealt with Dad's professional goods, his personal effects were fairly easy for us sibs to split up. (Our mother wanted us to have them all. His things were now too much of a painful reminder of his absence.) Those included a few objects he'd kept in a glass bowl on top of the living room credenza that were part of his everyday existence:

A class ring from Columbia, which he never removed. My sister took that.

His Seiko watch, which he was forever praising. ("Who'd buy an expensive watch when the Japanese make such a superior product? The Swiss can kiss their ass!") What were the odds that the Seiko would fit my brother's wrist perfectly?

His wallet, which was a tricky item for us to assign.

How strange to have someone's wallet, but not the person. You feel like calling the police and reporting yourself. My father's driver's license and his AAA, Social Security, credit, and insurance cards—all so important to him in his day-to-day life—rendered, in a flash, meaningless. Then we found the Holy Grail: a piece of paper, still in his wallet, that we'd all heard of countless times. It was a list of jokes that he always kept with him.

The list came about after he had accompanied my mother to one of her psychology conferences. The scheduled entertainment for the evening had canceled at the last minute. Aware that my dad knew his way around a joke or two, the attending Ph.D.s asked if my dad would mind stepping in and telling a few jokes to the crowd.

Mind stepping in?

For a man who dreamed of becoming a stand-up comedian (but happily settled for watching his daughter become one), this was easily one of the highlights of his life. And, as it was reported back to us, Pop slayed that crowd of shrinks. And if he were ever asked to perform a second time, Dad planned on being better prepared for his next show; hence, the list he kept in his wallet. Now I keep that little piece of paper in my wallet. (And don't think I won't pull it out the next time I'm stuck at a show.)

Then there were the clothes. For someone who seemed to wear the same six outfits his whole life, I don't know where all these items suddenly came from. I had the hardest time with the sweaters. My dad loved wearing sweaters. Anytime we ever wanted to raise the heat in the house, it was only a matter of seconds before we'd hear his standard rebuttal: "Just throw a good sweater on, and save some oil!"

While rummaging through my father's sweaters, I couldn't help but give them a good sniff and—voilà—there it was: his smell. That only made me want to get them out of the house as soon as possible. Because if they stayed too long, the Daddy Smell would soon be replaced by the smell of must and mothballs, and that wasn't him.

So off Dad's clothing went to Goodwill, another destination for his stuff that he would've appreciated. He grew up during the Depression (as we were so often reminded), and those Depression-era folks are very familiar with the concept of recycling, though their version has less to do with the environment and more to do with survival. Plus, Sy Leifer would definitely get a kick out of the fact that a leisure suit he bought thirty years ago from Syms in Roslyn,

Long Island, would be discovered and described as "vintage cool" by some hipster doofus one day soon.

And as I taped up the last sweater box, congratulating myself for appreciating Dad's things without getting too emotionally attached, I looked down in the closet, and I felt like I'd had the wind knocked out of me. I'd found the one thing I couldn't bring myself to put in the Goodwill box: the brown shoes, the ones with the rubber soles. The slip-ons he always wore.

They were all-purpose—for around the house, for going out, for when we took our three-mile walk around the neighborhood together. ("Dad, why don't you put on a pair of sneakers?" "*Sneakers?* Who needs sneakers?")

I was constantly on Dad's back to get rid of them, they were so comically old. In fact, I can't even say what brand they were because the lettering inside had long worn away. So old that they were from a shoe store that went belly-up ages ago, Miles Shoes. I pestered Dad all the time to spring for a new pair, but he would always say, "Why should I get a new pair when these work just fine?"

No wonder the concept of fashion does not compute with fathers. How can it, when clothing is reduced to either "working" or not?

The brown shoes . . . they just couldn't seem to add themselves to the Goodwill box. Instead, they sent a change of address card and moved to the back of Mom's closet. Nobody could decide what to do with them, and, when in doubt, do nothing, right? Isn't that the code of every procrastinator?

As I continued to pack up Dad's things, I asked myself: Out of everything, why the shoes? Why were they so hard to get rid of? Was it because they once held him, like they were kind of the trunk to his tree? Because his soul somehow seemed to stay in their soles? Was not getting rid of them some version of denial? Like, how can he be that far away if his shoes are still here?

There does come a point when you cry "uncle"—and finally have to admit that someone really is not coming back. For me, this happened at a specific moment during the week after my dad died.

As Jewish as my father was deep down, he and my mother had not belonged to a synagogue for a long time. So to perform the funeral, we hired what our tribe calls a Rent-A-Rabbi: one you don't know, but who officiates at a burial. But our Rent-A-Rabbi turned out to be quite different from what we had expected. Usually they just show up, ask a few routine questions, and get on with the task at hand, but ours seemed genuinely compassionate and engaged. After the ceremony, he gathered us all together and said, "If there's anything I can do to help you through this difficult time, please don't hesitate to ask. I am here for you one hundred percent. I will call you in a few days and check in."

"Sure," my mother said sarcastically after he left. "Once the check clears, adiós!"

Yet lo and behold, three days later, he did call. I answered the phone.

"Hello, this is your rabbi from the funeral," he said. "I'm just calling to see how your family's doing."

I was touched. "Thank you for calling, Rabbi!"

"How are you doing, sweetheart?"

"Right this moment, I'm doing okay. But honestly, Rabbi, two seconds from now, I could be a total wreck. My feelings change from moment to moment."

"Sweetheart, that is completely normal. Losing a parent is one of the most difficult passages of life. It's a roller coaster of emotions."

I nodded thoughtfully.

"Do you have any other concerns, darling?" he asked.

Feeling very safe and secure due to the rabbi's unexpected kindness, I decided to ask him the one question I'd actually been wrestling with for the previous seventy-two hours. "Rabbi, I do have a question. Where is my father now? I know he's not here, but he must be somewhere."

The rabbi sighed deeply and said, "Where is your *father now*? Oy, sweetheart, I'll be here all day! Can you put your sister on now, please?"

And did we laugh!

That Rent-A-Rabbi story quickly became running joke one million and one to the Leifer family, and the next time someone said something curt, impatient, or insensitive, one of us would race to be the first to say: "Yeah, now can you put your sister on, please?" The problem was, this was the first joke Dad wasn't there to share with us. And this reminded us—if we hadn't been 100 percent aware of it before—that Dad was really gone.

I'd always thought that when someone died, your relationship with that person was over. The end. Kaput. But it's not like that. Your relationship goes on, even though the other person isn't physically there. My Dad's there when I hear Stevie Wonder's "I Just Called to Say I Love You," a song he had a kooky kind of attachment to and whistled as he did crossword puzzles in the living room. He's with me when someone mentions disco, and I remember him valiantly trying to learn this new dance called the Hustle with me in 1975 as we listened to KC and the Sunshine Band. He's there when I buy a six-pack of individual orange juice containers ("Carol, what a waste. You're paying for the packaging with those small things! Do me a favor and buy the quart or the gallon size next time"). And he's there when I get a whiff of Jergens lotion, the cream he would put on his hands after doing the dishes. (And then you start to think things you never even thought when they were alive. Like, *Gee, that's an awfully femmie hand lotion for a man to use.*)

And we still have discussions. I have not made one important decision yet without talking it over with the old man first. I know he'd be happy with some choices I've made since his departure, others not so much. For instance, my recent decision to become a vegan would've inspired a lively discourse: "So you're deciding to give up meat completely? And dairy, too? Well, what the hell are you gonna eat? Nothing's left! All right, look, if that's what makes you happy, knock yourself out." (He said this last sentence countless times. It was his eventual response to almost everything.)

As the fourth anniversary of Dad's passing approaches,

I've decided that the next time I'm back home on Long Island, I'm going to finally drive over to Goodwill and donate the brown shoes. It's time. The shoes are ridiculously out of place in my mother's closet, now wedged between a pair of too-fancy slingbacks and Moroccan espadrilles. They're like the only guy you see sitting in a gynecologist's waiting room waiting for the wife to come back out.

It's what Pop would want, anyway. "Carol, *why deny someone the pleasure of these shoes?* Who knows how long they can go?" he'd ask.

We are not our things—my father was not his brown shoes. But I think I finally know why I had a hard time letting them go. Putting the shoes to rest meant ultimately putting Dad to rest, too. And I'm okay with that now. He liked a good rest.

And I see now that you don't have to be here when you're still everywhere.

Five Lessons of Animal Adoption

My favorite time of day is the few minutes before we all go to sleep. The sounds of peace abound:

The dishwasher hums in the kitchen. . . .

The baby monitor crackles lightly with static as our boy sleeps soundly upstairs. . . .

And the only sound from the maniacs is their soft and rhythmic breathing—their go buttons finally turned off at the end of a long day.

The maniacs would, of course, be our pack of seven rescue dogs. And as every dog lover knows, nothing is more beautiful (or calming, for that matter) than watching the easy rise and fall of those furry little bellies at rest. Chew toy squabbles tabled until tomorrow, with now only dreams of romping in fields flowering with Greenies.

As I look at them all splayed out over the different camps of our bedroom, I often wonder, *How the hell did one dog ever become seven?*

The short answers are:

I'm weak and very susceptible to big lonely eyes.

We've got the room.

I work from home.

And animals make me supremely happy in a way that nothing else does.

So let's start at the beginning. . . .

Our first adopted dog came from a Chihuahua rescue center in Burbank, California. We immediately noticed him—this guy with the floppy ears twice the size of his body—as soon as we came in. We glanced at the name card on his kennel, which read JULIUS. That was both my grandfather's and Lori's grandfather's name.

We inquired about Julius's story, and they told us that he had been found wandering outside USC when, just days earlier, we had laid to rest our good friend John Ritter—a proud USC alum. (So proud that his widow, Amy, commemorated John by having USC's marching band play at his memorial.)

And so begins:

LESSON #1: BE OPEN TO THE SIGNS

We played with Julius, took him for a little stroll, and then checked out a couple of different dogs as well. But we decided to think about it for a couple of days and head back

home. But before we left, something told me to go back in
and look for Julius one last time.

I knelt down by his kennel and asked point-blank,
"Should we come back for you, buddy?"

And he cocked his head with this sarcastic look like,
"I'm in a cage at a dog rescue. What do *you* think?"

But then, lest he give the impression that he was too
much of a smart-ass and squash the whole deal, Julius
reached out to me through the bars with his paw. And it was
then that I picked up the next lesson in animal adoption:

LESSON #2: THERE IS A MUTUAL "MEANT TO BE" MOMENT

And after a home check and the necessary paperwork had
been signed, the center brought our collective grandfathers'
namesake home to us.

Sometime later, we went back to the Chihuahua center
for our second rescue adventure, and this time met Linda—
an older dog they thought to be around six years old. Quiet
and terribly shy, this little apple-headed girl was nothing
more than a heat-seeking missile searching for a warm and
quiet lap. She had been deemed "unadoptable" by the city
shelter she'd come from (as in way too aggressive, with a
nonstop bark as well). But after a year of behavior modifi-
cation at the rescue, no such description could have been
further from the truth as she sat with us in an old beat-up
swing.

It was a typical summer San Fernando Valley day,
around 102 degrees, so we decided to take a break and get

some cold sodas. But sure enough, as we headed to the parking lot, we turned back around, and there was Linda seriously staring us down like we were two guests leaving a wedding before the bride has even made an appearance.

"Where you going, ladies?" she intimated with a quizzical look. "Was I crazy or were we not seriously hitting it off back here?"

So when we came back a little later a bit more hydrated, we decided to take that little girl home right then and there, being "preapproved" as we were from having adopted Julius two years earlier. But she left as Shelby, not Linda. You just know right away when the name doesn't fit. Besides, I like giving them new names. It officially commemorates their new and improved life starting with you.

So, as we said goodbye to the rescue center staff, Shelby safely tucked under Lori's arm, we discovered what we have since then always experienced when we adopt an animal and take them home that same day:

LESSON #3: IT ALL CHANGES IN THE CAR

Once that engine starts, animals know that things just got really good. Their expression, the way they hold themselves, their *everything* changes right before your eyes. Already feeling at home, Shelby propped herself up in Lori's lap, more than happy to share steering wheel duties on the ride back.

Our third rescue happened unexpectedly—but then, aren't they *all* unexpected after dog number two? We were at a Chanukah party at our friend Carole's (the ultimate animal lover who had been the one to turn us on to adopting). And who else happened to be there but the gal who ran the Chihuahua rescue center. She had brought some dogs along with her to meet a few prospective families, none of whom were supposed to be *us*. But then this little black-and-gray Chihuahua glued herself to Lori and me from the moment we got there.

She didn't even have a name (the rescue center being so overrun at holiday time that names were a luxury). As we took turns petting and holding her that evening at the party, from time to time Lori and I looked at each other from across the room with those silent looks that only couples can decipher. They said: "We can't. We shouldn't. We're good in the dog department." But all rational justifications went barreling out the window when we realized where Miss No Name was going home to that night if not with us.

And if anything made it easier, it was the first night of our Festival of Lights. (I've also found that when in doubt about adopting a dog, check the calendar. A holiday makes a great permission slip.) So along with some leftover latkes, we came home with little Maccabee—the brightest light in that year's menorah.

We decided to go hard-core for our next addition and so journeyed to a city shelter. It was an experience I wasn't quite prepared for. A city shelter is the pure embodiment of sadness and despair: rows and rows of animals whose eyes it is nearly impossible to look into because we know what they don't—that most will never get a second chance and that most will die for a crime that was not theirs. On top of that, you feel like every dog and cat in that shelter is yours. Having known what it's like to love and be loved by an animal, knowing the purity of their hearts and the unwavering fierceness of their devotion, there was, for us, no separating the souls inside those cages from the ones back home.

But then, in the midst of this horror story, I saw the coolest dude of cell block B—Shagster. Even though he was in a cage with four other crazy hyper dogs, this scruffy terrier was just lazily resting his head on crossed paws while letting out a big old yawn. The attitude just slayed me. Here he was in Treblinka, and he was just hangin', just chillin'. And I thought, if this dog could have this perspective *here,* I was definitely stressing about way too much stuff in my life. Which brings me to:

LESSON #4: LEARN SOMETHING TO FIX ABOUT YOURSELF
FROM YOUR ANIMAL

We glanced at Shagster's intake sheet and saw the reason he'd been impounded (which, to this day, still makes me flinch)—"Owner Surrender." Look, I know people get sick or old or financially can't handle their animals anymore. But don't they know there are no long-term stays at the city shelter? Couldn't they have tried looking for a no-kill rescue center to take their animal to?

It was pretty obvious, though, that his previous owner was no great shakes, as evidenced by Shagster's matted and completely overgrown hair. How could we not spring this dude from the joint? And his new name was a cinch to come up with. It was an Easter Sunday (another holiday, natch), and he looked exactly like Charlton Heston as Moses in *The Ten Commandments*. All he needed were two tablets in those paws, and it would have been a perfect match. So Heston he became. (And lo and behold, when he finally got that haircut, this boy got the makeover he had always deserved and became one handsome chap—the dog everyone now says would be a lock for a starring role on TV.)

Okay, lest you think we're absolutely whack, adoptees five and six weren't supposed to stay with us to begin with. You see, there was an APB email alert put out by a local rescue group stating that two senior Chihuahuas (sisters who were both fifteen) needed to get out of their shelter immediately because the next day was "E" day (the "E" being for "euthanasia"). Could someone get them out and foster them for a few days? (Lori had told me to take my address off those email lists, but *you* try sitting at a computer all day writing a book. A little life-and-death distraction is exactly what you need!)

I knew that getting one dog out of a shelter was tough enough—but two who were elderly and with cataracts to boot? Not the best odds. I have a real soft spot for the older ones. Dogs are our companions through thick and thin. But then why is it that when they get old, the "thick and thin" on our part gets a little murky?

I started strategizing immediately about the pitch I'd give to Lori. And of course, I ran to the calendar to see if mid-July had any major holidays. (When is that fake holiday Secretary's Day, anyway?!)

But word came back straightaway from my one and only: "No. Absolutely not."

"But it's just that—"

"I don't care. We have quite enough dogs, thank you. Besides, I'm on to you. I've already checked the calendar—and only the French celebrate Bastille Day, Carol!"

"But these dogs are not for us to keep. We're just a way station for the next few days until they find a permanent home for them."

I knew I had her there.

So the address to the North Central Animal Shelter was inputted into the GPS, and off we went. And once we got there, man, we had both never seen such sad and depressed dogs in our lives. Any other time we've approached a dog in a shelter, they've normally lit up, starved for attention. But not these little old ladies marooned in their cage for almost a month now. They couldn't even muster fake excitement. Instead, they looked like two miserable seniors who had been yanked from their condo in Miami Beach and unceremoniously dumped into a storage closet near the shuffleboard courts.

I must say, watching that big red "E" euthanasia placard fall into the trash as we left the shelter was a pretty amazing feeling. The fresh air outside was a welcome relief to the grandmas as we took them to the car. No complaints about a draft whatsoever. And when we got them home, we got an idea of how truly bonded they were. Each Chihuahua would freak if the other was gone too long. Lori warned me not to name them, reminding me they weren't staying long. But how can you ever resist naming them? That's one of the funnest parts! So—two sisters that would each easily take a bullet for the other? How could you name them anything but Cagney and Lacey?

About ten days later, I was home to get the message that Best Friends sanctuary had graciously accepted the old girls, and would let them live out the rest of their lives on their senior ranch in Utah. When Lori got home that night, I shared the good news. But then my better half, my voice of reason who endlessly puts the lid on my adopting entire shelters, actually said, "Over my dead body are those girls going anywhere."

How quickly these guys burrow their way into your heart. Thus . . .

LESSON #5: FOSTERING A DOG IS ONLY A HEARTSTRING AWAY FROM ADOPTING, SO MAKE THE DECISION CAREFULLY

Last month brought our latest addition purely by proxy. We went to the shelter to help some friends adopt their first dog, which is such a thrill. However, by now it should be pretty clear to everyone but us that you can't put Lori and me in a shelter for longer than two minutes without us leaving with something breathing. (Even if it's an overworked volunteer, they're still getting into that car!)

So, on this trip, we saw a little Yorkshire terrier puppy in a cage right near the entrance (because the shelter knew they had a winner). He was so impossibly adorable—the kind of dog that people cluelessly go to a pet store and easily shell out three grand for. His intake sheet said he was a stray, but I pulled myself away, really giving it the old college try.

"I have to have him."

What? Who said that?

"I'm absolutely smitten with that puppy," said Lori.

I couldn't believe it.

"Sweetheart, you're supposed to be the one with all her marbles here—the sane one to my relentless Dr. Dolittle."

"I just feel a connection to him. He reminds me of Murphy." (Lori's original dog, who had passed away.)

"I completely understand, but this puppy will be adopted in a second. If we take anyone, we should take one of the harder-luck dogs."

"What does it matter when he's still homeless?"

How could I argue with that one? Especially when my pocket calendar showed that Valentine's Day was at the end of the following week. (I never liked spending money on flowers much anyway.) And that was how Albert, named in honor of the great Mr. Einstein (since they shared the same wild hairstyle) came to complete our lucky seven.

Now, I've done some pretty spiritual things in my life. I've watched the sun come up over the Acropolis of Athens. I've hiked in the red rocks of Sedona, Arizona, and felt the power of the mystical vortices. I've even seen Barbra Streisand live on her farewell tour, *twice*. And yet none of these experiences even comes close to what I've felt adopting an animal.

This world feels so out of control at times—and you can feel absolutely powerless to have a hand in changing any of it. But when you adopt an animal, you create a little miracle. You right a little bit of what's gone wrong on this hare-brained planet of ours. You feel like every superhero rolled into one, because you took something dark and awful and made it light again.

There's so much we'll never know about our dogs. Who had them before us, and were they even *had* before? Were they kept outside or inside a house? And was it a house? What were they fed, or was there no one at all to feed them? Those questions will always be unanswered. But we do know that for a couple of our guys, somebody sure did a number on them. Shelby can still moonwalk better than Michael Jackson ever could. No creature learns that behavior from someone being too sweet to them. And Julius has this freaky reaction when either of us takes a belt off a hook in the closet. Of that, I shudder to think.

But that's the glory of animals. They are so elastically resilient. They truly can shake off their old life as if it were some bad dream. Happiness, joy, and trust are all possible again when animals have been given the unique gift of moving forward. What a pity so many of us two-leggers can't do the same, hung up and chained to our pasts as we so often are.

So . . . seven dogs. Yep, it's a lot of constantly counting them to make sure we've got them all. It's saying a million times a day, "Don't eat that!" And I've endured countless trips to the chiropractor from the contorted way I sleep, not wanting to—God forbid—disturb the canine royalty in our bed. And I can't use any more ChapSticks. They root them all out of my pants pockets eventually. Oh, yeah, and it's a lot of poop. (I had to laugh—when Lori and I made the decision to adopt a baby, the first thing people said who didn't know us was, "Get ready for all the poop you'll have to clean up!" And I was like, "Are you kidding? With seven dogs, a baby will be a *cakewalk*. The poop will at least be in a diaper now!")

But we wouldn't have it any other way. Especially when you finally come to realize that a dog's sole purpose here on earth is merely to love and be loved. Sure, I was fearful three dogs back that we'd be known as the "crazy Chihuahua ladies." But . . . too late.

Taking in these animals has shown me much. That small acts of love create the chain of a good life. That you can't save them all, but you can save a bunch. And that my lovely Lori can X them out with a Magic Marker in my day planner all she wants, but I'll still always know what holiday is just around the corner.

Class of '74

I've been to three high school class reunions so far, and I'm sure each one is universally typical. The ten-year one is just so you can see what everybody turned out looking like as an adult without the braces and bad skin (except for one poor guy). The twenty-year one is purely for the status report—spouse, job, house, salary. Very surface, *very* competitive (and I must say, I did very well). But as far as I'm concerned, you can skip 'em all until the thirtieth. The thirtieth reunion definitely kicks ass, even if that ass is somewhat saggy. It's like you're all just standing there, positively giddy, and . . .

"I'm here! I didn't get hit by a bus, or come down with a disease you can't spell, fall off a mountaintop, or trip on some concrete. I'm here! I didn't drive home after one too many mai tais, my hot-air balloon didn't pop, and I didn't

swallow anything tainted. So let's have a big round of ap-
plause for *me*!"

Besides, I find that you always have a particular fond-
ness for people your exact same age. The map of your life
has all the same reference points. Especially the pop culture
ones, because we didn't have ten thousand options like the
young pups do today. You remember all the same things.

Like when the Flintstones were on in prime time. And
when Topo Gigio, the little mouse, was on *The Ed Sullivan
Show*. And when there were only four TV channels and you
had to actually get up to change them. You remember when
girls had to wear a dress or skirt to school. There were no
seat belts in cars. Popcorn was made on the stove. And that
the only thing that got shot at your school was your year-
book picture.

You even remember how you didn't have the foggiest
notion of what Steely Dan looked like, and didn't care, because when you heard their music, it didn't matter. You remember when Michael Jackson's talent was scary, rather
than what *he looks like* being scary. How you knew every
word to the album *Tapestry* by Carole King in ninth grade—
that is, until you scratched it unmercifully because you
played it on your record player an ungodly number of times
and had to go out and buy a new copy. And what about
Kitty Carlisle, Durwood Kirby, Soupy Sales, Castro Con-
vertibles—even Dippity-do! No need to struggle to explain
them to anyone at your thirtieth. It's your club. Show 'em
some ID with your date of birth (or show your AARP card),
and you're in!

There you can reminisce about things like the "long-distance trick" that everybody was in on at the time, passed down purely by word of mouth. How when you went away and your parents wanted to know that you'd arrived safely, they told you to call home collect and ask for yourself. Then one of them would answer the phone and tell the operator that you weren't there and hang up. And finally they could have a good night's sleep knowing that you'd gotten to Grandma's in Florida okay. (Plus they saved twenty cents.)

Not to mention the historical events we witnessed as one. When John Kennedy was shot, we were all only tadpoles, but I'm sure each one of us would say that we remember it as if it were yesterday. For us, it happened at a particularly unique age. Seven years old was quite a perch to view that event from. Too young to be affected by it emotionally, of course, but certainly old enough to take it all in and process it.

Being sent home from our second-grade class at school was certainly a tip-off that something monumental had happened. And then feeling this vast quiet at home and in the neighborhood. To see both my parents crying, and about something not family-related, was definitely a trip, too.

Watching someone even younger than us at the time be intimately involved, Kennedy's son, John, or "John John" as he was nicknamed, certainly fascinated us. The image of his salute at the funeral had a profound impact on the world, but I think it impacted children especially.

(FYI, that experience also gave me a new appreciation of

the seven-year-old mind. I will always know that little minds are capable of gathering great concepts.)

And what about at thirteen watching a man land on the moon? The scope of that event. The swelling excitement and pride that no one was immune to (especially compared to your average person today, who doesn't even know when a space shuttle launch is). It felt like humans were real-life superheroes. What will my son experience that will even come close to that? (And yet, I'm sure he will. Each generation has their "moon walk" moment, although we like to think that ours was the only one.)

Yes, the night of my thirtieth reunion sure was a blast. We all stayed till well after four in the morning, as I recall. Laughing, palling around, and singing along to all those great songs, *our* songs. How nice it was to remember when "Takin' Care of Business" by Bachman-Turner Overdrive was not the Office Depot theme song. And when Carly Simon's "Anticipation" didn't make you think of that Heinz ketchup commercial. But I especially remember when *it* came on. "Tapestry." And it suddenly got silent. No singing along this time . . .

My life has been a tapestry
Of rich and royal hue . . .

How odd that this song, which we sang along to mindlessly thirty-three years ago like teenage robots, was a song about the very stage we found ourselves at now in our lives. (And how did Carole King in her twenties write so eloquently about something that was so beyond her years?)

So if I were you, I'd definitely skip the reunion invites until number thirty. Because you leave the thirtieth not comparing crow's feet with the girl who played flute next to you in band. Or worrying who makes more money, you or your old lab partner, who threw up when you had to dissect a frog. No, you leave with one overwhelming emotion—gratitude. You finally get that whatever age you are is just the right age. Because the sum total of all those events and experiences have actually made the person that is you. (And made the *collective* you, too.) Your life *is* this tapestry now, of rich and royal hue.

Would I still like to be younger? Sometimes. (My pants sure wish I was.) But would I trade any of it now to be someone else? And miss the thrill of getting a telegram? Miss riding my bike without having to wear a helmet? Miss doing this brand-new dance called the Twist? Miss looking something up on microfilm in the library? (Okay, maybe I don't miss that one so much.) Miss seeing an original hippie? Not on your life, pal.

Buried or Not, Here I Come

The fight started in the waiting room of the lawyer's office. And let me tell you, if you're going to fight, that's really not the best place to do it. Before the incident, the guy in the suit sitting next to me simply wanted to finish that day's *Wall Street Journal,* and the older woman in the corner wearing the sensible pumps was nose-deep into the latest Jodi Picoult novel.

But tensions always run high when you're about to sign important legal documents, although it didn't seem that way moments before on the car ride over when Lori and I were bickering about which XM satellite radio station to settle on. Why listen to "Come On, Eileen" on the eighties channel for the millionth time (I mean, come *on* already, Eileen!)

when Dr. Oz is talking about the correct shape your poop should be on the Oprah and Friends channel?

Lori and I were at the estate lawyer's to sign my will. Now, it's clear that no one wants to think about dying. (Proof positive: the huge popularity of drugs and alcohol.) So for years, it went something like this in my head:

I don't want to make my will. Eww—no. I'd much rather find Beatles memorabilia on eBay. Or get one of those cool new massages with the hot stones. Or buy something I don't need online at Brookstone that will make my life easier. Did you hear that, Will? My life, which I'm very much in the midst of, thank you very much!

Besides, didn't the estate lawyers get the memo informing them that I'm *never going to die*? The attorneys can call it a serious state of denial, but I prefer to think of it as a deep faith in the world of science. (If they can clone a sheep, for God's sake, making me live forever can't be all that far behind!)

Also, in general, I'm quite adept at putting things off—just ask the nineteen boxes of pictures I've yet to put in photo albums since 1982. But procrastination is a young woman's game, and as the birthday candles grow in number until there's very little cake left in sight, death plants itself right in your face like an ex-girlfriend with a prior history of stalking who's just been jilted by text message. On top of all that, add a child into the mix, and suddenly there's nowhere left to hide.

So I finally hunkered down to write my will. And it went a lot easier than I had imagined. The "Where will my stuff go?" part turns out to be real easy when you're in a long-term relationship, because it all goes to your partner. (Let me amend that to "*happy* long-term relationship," because the years together don't mean squat if the will writer feels that your time together has been sheer hell.)

Boy, the headaches I saved leaving it all to the missus. Suddenly off the table were all those questions that I never wanted to deal with. (Like, "Which comedian buddy do I leave the framed cue cards to—the ones with the banter between Bob Hope and Milton Berle from a young comedians' TV special I did with them?") Fantastic! Let the widow figure it out!

So I thought this signing thing at the estate lawyer's office would not only be a breeze, but we could probably even squeeze in a lunch nearby at one of our favorite vegan joints as well. But not so, as I soon found out while Lori leafed through the will.

"Did you know it says here, Carol, that you want to be buried in Queens?" Lori asked.

"Yeah. At the cemetery where my dad is now and my mother will be."

"But my father already bought us a burial spot."

"He did? Where?"

"At the Jewish cemetery in West L.A., where all my family is."

"That cemetery near the airport? But you've always told me that place doesn't have any more room left in the ground."

"Yes, that's true. So my dad bought us a crypt in the mausoleum."

"*Crypt? Mausoleum?* Did he also happen to buy one for Elvira, Mistress of the Dark?"

The woman formerly transfixed by Jodi Picoult suddenly peered over her reading glasses, sensing some real, not fictional, excitement brewing in the air.

"I thought I told you this," Lori said.

"No, you didn't. Wait a second, 'crypt' as in those long drawers like they put your uncle Max in when we went to his funeral?"

Lori nodded.

"No way," I said. "I'm not winding up in that morbid file cabinet. How are people going to find me? With a folder tab from Staples? No, thanks."

"But isn't it important to you that we be buried together?"

The guy in the suit next to me squirmed uncomfortably in his seat and ahemmed loudly as he turned the page of the financial section.

"Honestly, no," I said. "Is it important to you?"

"Very much so," Lori said heatedly. "I can't believe, Carol, that you didn't even bother to run this by me before putting it in the papers!" she said a little too loudly.

Then sensing the awkward vibe of the waiting room, I suggested, "Lori, maybe we should just table this until we're inside the office."

"Nuh-uh," Lori said, on a mission. "Did you see what this gonif [Yiddish for "thief"] charges an hour? No, we've got to settle this *now*."

And even though her book was covering her face, I felt a big smile blooming from the Jodi Picoult lady.

I was forthright in my explanation:

"Lori, I just feel that: (a) I want to be underground when I'm dead—that's where the dead people go, and (b) we're going to be *dead*. It's not like we're gonna be catching up every day like two yentas nudging each other out there saying, 'Honey, did you see who just got here? Debbie Markowitz! And she looks fantastic, too!' "

"But couples are supposed to be buried together," Lori said.

"Really? Is that in an etiquette book somewhere? Besides, I don't want to be buried in California. I want to be in New York."

"But you've lived here for almost twenty years."

"I know, but New York is my home."

"Well, you're the one who said it, Carol. You're going to be dead anyway, so how will you know what city you're in?"

The man in the suit chuckled audibly at that retort as the receptionist came out and called him in.

"It's just weird, Carol," Lori said. "To be buried separately? Just plain weird."

"Why don't we just get you a plot in New York alongside me?"

"Because I don't want to be buried in New York away from *my* family. And you know how much I hate the cold, Carol!"

I nervously checked my watch. Where was that lawyer?! I knew this discussion couldn't go on much longer with the meter ticking. And then suddenly, as I was wondering if I had put on antiperspirant that morning, the receptionist came out to get us.

As it turned out, we didn't wind up talking about our "end" plans any further once we were inside the lawyer's office—we knew we had said everything we needed to say in the waiting room. But we did cover all the other uncomfortable bases, things like that messy "What would happen if we both died in a plane crash?" mishegoss. And I also got a big "Absolutely" from the lawyer to the question "And anything in the will can always be changed at any time, correct?" That seemed to be the most important detail to cover at that point.

So we left the attorney's office. And we had time to hit that vegan place after all. But while sharing our soy tuna melt, I thought about how the afternoon had gone so differently than planned. Earlier, I'd thought I'd be basking in praise and scoring major points with my ladylove as I gladly left all my earthly posessions to her. Ah, no such luck.

But since that day, Lori and I have never talked about the subject again. Not because of any anger or hurt feelings, but just because we know we're at a standstill. But I'm not worried. Believe me, which side of the family we'll be spending the forever family reunion with will be broached again.

In the meantime, I still anxiously await every Tuesday's edition of *The New York Times* and devour that science section for the permanent waiver from the grim reaper. Any day now, I'm telling you, our tiff will all have been for naught and the only thing we'll need to agree on is where and what condo we're going to buy to spend our next hundred years together.

Trust me, with Apple hawking a new iPhone every six months, they're sure to be the first ones out there with that eternal life vaccine. And if I have to stay in California for my final resting spot, then so be it. But next time I'm at that cemetery near the airport, I'll make it my mission to find a freewheelin' grave digger who won't look askance at a hundred bucks for a couple of spots under the 405 freeway.

Creating a Jew

I had always felt like a Jew. I know most, if not all, of the words to *Fiddler on the Roof.* I'm no stranger to a nice piece of babka. And when I call someone a mensch, I know I'm saying so much more than "nice guy."

But then came this problem . . .

I didn't feel like a *whole* Jew.

And it became more and more apparent each year when I went to temple for High Holiday services. Suddenly, for such a Jew, I felt clueless. Hebrew still looked like spilled ink to me, and the prayers sounded like Bob Dylan was singing them with a head cold. And even though I was aware that the prayer book was read backward, I felt somewhat like a fraud—like what was inside me didn't really match up to the outside. (Similar to people who have those alarm-company signs posted on their lawns but don't actually have the security systems.)

Growing up on Long Island, I had only gone to temple briefly as a small child. I don't remember much, except that during services when I heard the kaddish (the mourner's prayer), it sounded a lot like they were talking about one of my favorite foods: "The Yish Kebab, the Shish Kebab." But then my father ended his temple membership the year after my grandfather passed away, which happened when I was around six.

You see, my dad had had a very strict Orthodox education as a child and it had soured him. He recounted a lot of unhappy memories when he was a little boy of having to be in shul for hours on end, when all he yearned for was to go outside and play. And then there was the mandated Hebrew memorization and learning drills run by taskmaster teachers that were never to be interrupted, even if the children were tired or had to relieve themselves. It wasn't hard to understand how he had become very resentful of it all.

And yet, if I was asked for one word to describe my father, it would be "Jewish." Somehow the joy of his faith still shone through. He spoke glowingly over the years of his family, like how they would sing Jewish songs all together at home. And there were the endless raves about his mother's cooking—all homemade from scratch. In fact, his mouth would still water from just the pure memory of the hamantaschen she made for Purim. Not to mention the gefilte fish she crafted by herself, with the carp swimming in the one bathtub in their home. And, oh, the homemade schmaltz (chicken fat) they used to slather on thick slices of her just-out-of-the-oven challah bread.

Dad had learned Yiddish from my immigrant grandparents and spoke it so beautifully that patients who came into his optical office from the "old country" would ask him where he was from. That made him very proud.

So a few years ago, at Rosh Hashanah (New Year) service, there was a pamphlet on the seats of the synagogue advertising the adult b'nai mitzvah class that was about to start. Like me, Lori had had a minimal Jewish education as well (ironically, at this same temple). So, both in our forties, we figured "better late than never" and decided to get bat mitzvahed.

For twenty-four Thursday nights, from seven to nine-thirty, we went to class. And I got a real kick out of the fact that, at this age, I could turn down invitations with "I'm sorry, but I have my bat mitzvah lessons that night." Lori's aunt, uncle, and cousin also joined the course, so it made it a real family affair.

And, other than that homework and studying can still be a real drag, I learned a lot—like tons of history that I had never been aware of. (With, of course, a central theme being people keep chasing our people out of wherever we want to be!) I also learned the Hebrew alphabet, and how to read the language as well.

I can't begin to tell you how exciting it was when I finally read my first Hebrew word out in the real world. Lori and I were back in New York over Thanksgiving, and I sounded out a word on a deli sign.

"B-b-b-b-bosher."

"I think you might mean 'kosher,' Carol," my older brother, Marv, said. "But good job!" (Those *b* and *k* letters are awfully close.)

I also brought the temple prayer book home, as I was trying to familiarize myself with the Shabbat (Sabbath, Friday night) service, and went over some of it with my father. Even though he was in poor health at the time and hadn't been to shul in years, just the mention of a prayer or a snippet of a song and he could recite the entire passage perfectly. I guessed it would always be a part of him, regardless of his childhood experience.

But the best thing about the b'nai mitzvah class did not come from a book. It was the new relationships we forged with the rabbi and cantor who taught the course. Before this experience, the expression "cool rabbi" or "funny cantor" would have been an oxymoron to me. Ron (yes, the rabbi wanted us to call him Ron) was around our same age and an intelligent, interesting, cyclin'-lovin' guy. (There's also a rabbi named Spike at the temple!) And the cantor, Nate (a real "tummler," as is said in Yiddish), gave me a run for my money in the jokes department. Every Thursday night, he'd greet me with a "So did you hear the one about . . . ?" Judaism wasn't supposed to be like this.

There's also the fact that the temple, being reform, accepted me and Lori as a couple, so much so that the rabbi (sorry, *Ron,* it's still hard to make that change) actively campaigned throughout the course for Lori and me to get married, and he continues to this day. Maybe the dude just likes wedding cake, but it was and is sweet.

The most difficult part of the process, however, was memorizing my haftorah portion, which each person reads aloud to the congregation at the ceremony. Nate the cantor (shouldn't every cantor's name be Nate?) put each person's segment on a CD, so for weeks beforehand I would drive around furiously trying to learn my portion as best I could.

And three weeks before the b'nai mitzvah, after I had been playing my CD virtually nonstop on a weekend ride to Laguna Beach and back, I got the call that Dad had died.

I went back to New York for the funeral and to sit shivah for a week with my family. When I got home, my father's health-care aide confided that near the end, in his delirium my father would often chant Jewish prayers. And I wondered, had we somehow channeled each other, my dad and I? Had my endless repetition of the haftorah CD overlapped somewhere out there in the universe with my father's recitations, woven so deep inside him that they were part of his unconscious fabric?

But when I stood at my father's graveside and we said the kaddish prayer, I didn't have to mumble it like all the times before. I was able to say it and know the meaning of each word. And for the year following his death, saying my old "shish kebab" prayer every week at Shabbat services consoled me in a way that nothing else did. It's quite an extraordinary passage—not at all somber or dreary, and it doesn't mention death even once. Quite the contrary, it is a joyful exaltation of G-d and an affirmation of the worthwhile nature of life. And I found that in such a state of mourning, that's exactly where you need to be pointed. The last thing you want to do is dwell in the darkness, even though your heart is leading you that way. I clearly understand now its power through the generations.

I returned to Los Angeles, and two weeks later was our graduation, the b'nai mitzvah ceremony. When I was back in New York for the funeral, my mother had found something quite special up in the attic—my father's tallis—the one that he'd worn during his bar mitzvah in 1930. So I wore my father's tallis that incredible day and it felt like his hands on my shoulders.

But I must admit, for someone who's done so much live performing in clubs and on television, I was way more nervous than I'd expected. I even caught a surprised glance from Ron when my hand noticeably quivered holding the yad (the pointer that is used to read the Torah scroll) during the haftorah portion of the ceremony. Funny how you put G-d into the house and the butterflies fly up into a completely new ether.

We then each had to make a personal statement, and I told a story about my father from years ago when, while at the airport, we passed a man asking for money. My dad was not the type to give to people like this. Not that he wasn't compassionate, but I knew he felt giving money was just a Band-Aid to a much bigger problem. But in this instance, the man asking for money was wearing a yarmulke, so this brought my father to a dead halt.

He approached the man and asked, "So what's your Jewish name?"

After the man answered convincingly, my father then proceeded to "pop-quiz" him in Judaism 101. Finally, when the guy wound up with a B-plus overall on the lightning round of questions, my dad handed the man twenty dollars.

"Always be extra mindful to your own," my father said to me as we walked on. "It's a shanda [shame] that fella wound up like that."

I felt that story said a lot, not only about my dad, but much about the legacy of our people.

We had a big party that night to celebrate our b'nai mitzvah—Lori, me, her aunt, uncle, and cousin. It certainly was a great feeling to have a goal like this and see it completed. (My only surprise was that I didn't receive one fountain pen as a gift. FYI: Unlike weddings, there's no time limit on sending b'nai mitzvah gifts. I'm kidding, of course. Maybe.)

Then, three years later (our Jewish ID cards a bit more official now), a new Jewish task presented itself when Lori and I adopted our son. But it seemed that this time we needed to start from square one in creating this new little Jew.

We adopted our son at ten months old with his birth name intact—Bruno. We had fully planned on changing his name to Shane in honor of my father, Seymour. But when we finally laid eyes on our Latino son, the name Shane honestly felt ridiculous. But before we could officially give him his

Hebrew name, Shmuel (the same as my father's), we needed to complete two steps of conversion.

The first step was to have him circumcised. Normally this takes place on the eighth day after a son's birth. But when you adopt a child who is already ten months old, it becomes quite a different proposition and requires a hospital procedure—with anesthesia. And a lot of people don't want to go through all the tsuris. But we knew in the long run it would be for the best, for health reasons and for getting to that all-important Jewish finish line. (Besides, what's a Jew without a little tsuris anyway?)

We were lucky enough to find a great doctor to do the circumcision—the head (ahem) of pediatric urology at UCLA, who had performed the procedure umpteen times, so we felt confident. The doc was not only a urologist but a certified mohel. (Only in L.A., right?)

As it turned out, Bruno was a real trouper. Yes, he had no idea what lay ahead of him that morning in the prep room as he flirted with the nurses and played with their stethoscopes. When they carried him back to the operating room, Bruno was laughing and giggling without a care in the world. He was like, "Come on, what could they possibly do to me back there? *It's not like they're going to chop off half my shmeckle or anything!*"

Finally, when we were all together in the operating room—the mohel-surgeon, ourselves, my mother-in-law, my sister-in-law, and Ron the rabbi (as always) there to officiate—our son joined the covenant. Even with all of us wearing scrubs and face masks, and against the constant *beep, beep* drone of those medical machines, it was as powerful an experience as I'd ever felt.

(Though, when we took that bandage off Bruno ten days later, it was a day I never want to relive—and I'm pretty sure our son would agree. I'm positive Bruno was thinking, *You people sure don't make it easy to become a member of this tribe.*)

The next step was immersing Bruno in a mikvah, which happened a month after he had healed from the circumcision. The mikvah (which looks like a miniature swimming pool) took place at the University of Judaism here in Los Angeles. The ceremony was witnessed by three rabbis, who I'd heard beforehand usually tend to be on the older side. (All I know is, one of them told me on which side Moses had parted the Red Sea.)

Lori and I got into our bathing suits, and, taking our naked Bruno into the mikvah with us, we prepared to dunk him three times. (Okay, so maybe they gave us a free pass on the third dunk, as Bruno had swallowed a fair amount of water on the second one, but regardless, we did it.)

Finally, three weeks later, we had Bruno's brit chayim (naming ceremony). For the occasion, Bruno's aunt Linda made him a little yarmulke with a Noah's ark theme, in honor of all the animals who share our life. And damn, did Bruno sure look sweet wearing it as Rabbi Ron took him into the fold. Thus Bruno officially became Shmuel Chaim Baruch, in honor of my father and Lori's grandfather (with the added Baruch meaning "blessing" in Hebrew). So we had our dressed-up moment with friends and enjoyed a nice spread afterward. (Because what's a Jewish "moment" without the presence of some lox and bagels?)

And now, a year and a half later, our boy attends the temple day school. Recently, they called us in to discuss Bruno's continuing at the school next year. After discussing our hopes and goals for him during the next twelve months, they invited us to look around the school while it was in session, welcoming us to peek our heads into any class we liked.

We stopped by a class of what looked to be kids about five years old. They were singing a Jewish song (one I wasn't familiar with) and clapping along and having a good time as only children can. And while I pictured Bruno sitting there in that same spot a few years from now, singing happily and enjoying himself all the while getting his Jewish education, somewhere my father was kvelling. Taking that first step of faith with fun and laughter, not rigidity and discipline? Becoming a Jew as a joyous experience? What a concept! Could the path that had veered off so badly for my father as a child now find the right direction for our son? Maybe it just took a couple of generations to finally get it right.

And though it happened thirty-five years later than usual, I'm now so proud to say that I became a bat mitzvah and along the way rediscovered my Jewish heritage. (I knew I put it somewhere.) Yes, there are still those ever pesky questions: Did G-d create the universe in six days? (Hey, it takes me a lot longer than that to put together a garage sale.) Why did G-d turn Lot's wife into a pillar of salt? Didn't he know how many of us Jews suffer from high blood pressure? Yes, many events in the Bible sound straight out of a David Blaine special. But I'm not going to be the one who says they *didn't* happen, that's for sure.

But I do know this: I am a link in a long, long chain, and that chain is strong and unbreakable. We are mindful of our own. Our son is in that chain now. And someday, his child will be, too. This oh-so-brief stay here on earth makes a lot more sense now in that context.

So Lori and I were a little late to the party, but the point is, we're *at* the party. For our son to become a Jew, it seemed we had to start from scratch. But that's okay. As my father would easily tell you about his mother's homemade cooking:

Anything made from scratch is always that much more delicious.

Been There, Done That

Turning fifty was a mindblower. All I could think about was the sheer volume of stuff that has happened in my life so far—and so many were things that I had always been fearful of.

For example, I've missed a flight. I've also gone to Kennedy airport for a flight, only to discover it actually departed from LaGuardia. And I've gotten on the wrong flight and realized it so late that I wasn't allowed to get off the plane to get on the right flight. (Do you have any idea what *four hours* going in the wrong direction is like? With a gig to still make that night?)

I've had my purse stolen easily eight times in my life. (Thank you, New York City!) And one time, the crook took my house keys out of my purse, found my address on my driver's license in my wallet, and then ransacked my apartment, too.

I've had my share of car troubles. Like a flat tire on a crowded L.A. freeway during afternoon rush hour with no cell phone. And another time, I was waiting so long for AAA to come and had to pee so badly that I left the car, walked over to my cousin's house, who wasn't home at the time, and peed on her back lawn. (She won't know this until she reads this book. Oops.) Mom *was* right. Always carry a pocket pack of tissues with you everywhere you go.

I've been pulled over by the police on suspicion of drunk driving after not having had anything to drink. Apparently, I was doing a lot of weaving while trying to open a PayDay candy bar. The cop made me recite the alphabet on the sidewalk, but I was so freaked out, and with all the cars whizzing by, I actually had some trouble.

I've lost tons of things. Like my glasses in Belize. And an expensive bracelet on the beach that my mother let me borrow. (I never thought that one of those nut jobs roaming around with a metal detector would become my new best friend.) And sets of keys? Countless times. I once had to go searching for a pair on the Back to the Future ride at Universal Studios between seatings.

I've had a biopsy. I've had not just one but three colonoscopies. I've gotten a killer yeast infection in Aruba. One in Manchester, England, too. (Though, I would skip a gyno visit over there if possible. The Brits don't use the American "stirrups" system so for the exam they basically lay you out on a table on a bad sheepskin car seat cover. You feel like a three-quid whore.)

I've been taken down off a mountain by the ski patrol. I've ridden a hydroplane (until I found out there were alligators in the water below and made the boat turn around). I've tripped on my face in front of a large group of people. I've even blanked while doing stand-up on live television.

I've been questioned by customs after an overseas trip to verify that I'd declared everything I was supposed to when I hadn't. I've made a bad investment in a dot-com. We had a beach house that had rats. I've been in two car accidents. I've gotten divorced. I saw my father dead. A coyote bit my dog. I turned forty. I turned *fifty*. I once weighed 159 pounds. I had to write my will. I've gotten locked out of my house three times. I've been fired more times than I like to remember. I've been in an earthquake. I was turned down by *The Tonight Show* sixteen times when Johnny Carson hosted. (But they said yes on the seventeenth time!) I had to admit I was falling in love with a person of the same sex. I've gotten the worst haircut of my life. (My bangs were actual quarter-inch wisps—I looked like I had escaped from a Czechoslovakian loony bin.)

I was certain I was about to die once on a Greek vacation while in a ferryboat from Mykonos to Páros during a violent rainstorm. So certain that I wrote a note to leave behind.

And you know what? It's all been okay.

You see, the beauty of getting older that nobody tells

you is that so many of the fears you had when you were younger have already happened. And you've figured them out and weathered each one like a champ.

The bogeyman finally comes out from under the bed, and he's old and fat and just wanted a cookie.

Aging turns out to be a "glass half-empty" sort of character. The sagging, the wrinkles, the march toward death—that's all it goes on and on about, ad nauseam. But what it *should* be bragging about is how prepared and confident it's made you for all the twists and turns of life. I can enjoy so many more things now, and in such a fuller way, because the bulk of that pesky fear factor is gone.

Okay, so I've still never fainted. And I've never broken a leg or an arm or anything, for that matter. And you can't get on a wrong flight anymore, not with the übersecurity they've got going since 9/11. But whatever you got, life, bring it on! It'll be hard to throw me for a loop—especially when I've had drinks and dinner with most of the loops already.

Yes, I'm quite the threat all by myself. But throw in a pocket pack of tissues, and I'm downright invincible!

Acknowledgments

It's not easy having a writer in your life.

You get *this* a lot: "Hey, got a second to hear a line I'm thinking of?" Or "What the hell . . . Do you have five minutes, ten tops, to read this piece I wrote?" Believe me, it really becomes a pain.

So with great appreciation, I'd like to acknowledge these fine friends and family members who stuck with me through this long and exciting process: Beth Lapides and Greg Miller of Un-Cab, who started me off on this road. Rob Weisbach, for nudging me in this direction. My agent, Daniel Greenberg, my "squeaky wheel." Maggie and Jimmy at Sit 'N Spin— your bookings made me do my work. Wendy Hammers of Tasty Words. My dear friends Jon Macks, Dave Boone, Beth Armogida, Bruce Vilanch, David Schneiderman and Bob

Nitkin Schneiderman, Ricky Strauss, Marc Shaiman, Scott Wittman, Jessica Seinfeld, Julie Silver, Sherrie Krantz, Jane Gennaro, Pat Dengler, Sue Kolinsky, Judy Orbach, Pat Buckles, Cathy Rath, and Sue DeLuca. An extra-special shout-out to my buddy Bill Kelley. Family who helped enormously: Jane Lampert, Linda and Jeff Wolf, and Kathy Klein. A giant thank-you to those friends (who also happen to be huge celebs) who took the time to read my manuscript and give me such great feedback: Bill Maher, Jerry Seinfeld, Larry David, Ellen DeGeneres, Chris Rock, Garry Shandling, Rosie O'Donnell, and Margaret Cho. A huge love offering to Bruce Tracy, my editor, who took a chance on me and calmed me down more than once with "You're overthinking this, Carol!"

And to my sweet Lori and my funny B-Man: Thank you for understanding my long hours in "the bubble." You are my lucky stars.

About the Author

CAROL LEIFER is an accomplished stand-up comedian and an Emmy-nominated writer and producer for her work on such television shows as *Seinfeld, The Larry Sanders Show, Saturday Night Live,* and the Academy Awards. She has starred in several of her own comedy specials, which have aired on HBO, Showtime, and Comedy Central. Her "big break" came when David Letterman unexpectedly showed up one night at The Comic Strip in New York City and caught Carol's show. His visit led to her making twenty-five guest appearances on *Late Night with David Letterman.* Carol has also been seen on *The Tonight Show, Real Time with Bill Maher, Late Night with Conan O'Brien,* and *The Oprah Winfrey Show.* She starred in and created the WB sitcom *Alright Already.* She lives in Santa Monica with her partner, their son, and their seven rescue dogs.

www.carolleifer.com

About the Type

This book was set in Sabon, a typeface designed by the well-known German typographer Jan Tschichold (1902–74). Sabon's design is based upon the original letter forms of Claude Garamond and was created specifically to be used for three sources: foundry type for hand composition, Linotype, and Monotype. Tschichold named his typeface for the famous Frankfurt typefounder Jacques Sabon, who died in 1580.